FREE
TIME

This is a volume in the
Arno Press collection

GROWING OLD

Advisory Editor
Leon Stein

See last pages of this volume
for a complete list of titles

FREE
TIME

Challenge
to
Later
Maturity

Conference on Aging

*Edited by Wilma Donahue, Woodrow W. Hunter,
Dorothy H. Coons, and Helen K. Maurice*

ARNO PRESS

A New York Times Company
New York • 1980

Editorial Supervision: BRIAN QUINN

———

Reprint Edition 1980 by Arno Press Inc.

Copyright © by the University of Michigan 1958
Reprinted by permission of The University of Michigan Press
Reprinted from a copy in the Library of the University of Illinois

GROWING OLD
ISBN for complete set: 0-405-12813-4
See last pages of this volume for titles.

Manufactured in the United States of America

———

Library of Congress Cataloging in Publication Data

Conference on Aging, 10th, University of Michigan, 1957.
   Free time.

   (Growing old)
   Reprint of the ed. published by the University of
Michigan Press, Ann Arbor.
   Conference was sponsored by the Division of Geron-
tology of the University of Michigan.
   Includes index.
   1. Aged--Recreation--Congresses. 2. Leisure--
Congresses. 3. Time allocation--Congresses. I. Dona-
hue, Wilma T. II. Michigan. University. Division of
Gerontology. III. Title. IV. Series.
[GV184.C63 1980]   790.1'926   79-8667
ISBN 0-405-12807-X

FREE TIME

Challenge to Later Maturity

FREE TIME

Challenge
to
Later
Maturity

*ited by Wilma Donahue, Woodrow W. Hunter,
rothy H. Coons, and Helen K. Maurice*

THE UNIVERSITY OF MICHIGAN PRESS

ANN ARBOR

Foreword

There is being produced today, as a by-product of modern technology, an ever-increasing supply of the commodity of free time—time that is not and need not be devoted to paid employment. The abundance of this new leisure raises the vital issue of its wise investment by society and by the individual. Because free time is available in larger measure to middle-aged and older adults, the responsibility for the solution to the problem of its meaningful use lies largely in the hands of the older age groups.

The University of Michigan Tenth Anniversary Conference on Aging, held June 24 to 26, 1957, was devoted to a consideration of free time as a major challenge of the later years of life. In this book is offered a selection of the distinguished papers presented at the conference. Questions basic to the understanding of the changing societal patterns and the employment of unpaid time along with suggested uses for satisfying leisure experience offer readers practical guidance for meeting the personal challenge of the gift of abundant leisure. In the Preface, Clark Tibbitts, initiator of the Michigan Conferences on Aging and a long-time and close student of social change as it relates to the aging of the population, makes crystal clear the urgent need for the appreciation and acceptance of leisure as one of the great positive values of modern society.

The Division of Gerontology, the Extension Service, and the Summer Session wish to acknowledge the assistance and inspiration afforded by the several University professional schools and institute departments, the Michigan state agencies concerned with aging, the Michigan State Medical Society, the United States Department of Health, Education, and Welfare, and The Fund for Adult Education, which joined the University of Michigan in the planning and offering of the Tenth Anniversary Conference on Aging. To the authors of the several chapters the University is especially indebted for their willingness to undertake assignments in the new and pioneering field of leisure and aging.

Wilma Donahue

June 26, 1957

Preface

With the Tenth Anniversary Conference, these annual University of Michigan Conferences on Aging have come to a full cycle. Over a period of a decade, the University has sponsored this series of exploration, which has now extended into every major phase of what we term the phenomenon of our aging population.

These conferences have been notable in other respects than merely the systematic way in which they have examined the field. To a quite extraordinary degree they have attracted men and women of high professional standing in a variety of related fields, and also an increasing number of vigorous lay people seeking to become more useful citizens in their own communities. If I may borrow a term from anthropology, I should say that the level of these conferences has consistently drawn to Ann Arbor the culture creators among us—that is, the restless and imaginative individuals who find themselves constantly striving to improve the environment—in this case to develop a favorable climate for our new generation in middle age and later maturity.

Furthermore, these conferences have made brilliant use of the concept of audience participation. Year after year, the discussion groups have become an eager exchange of ideas and concrete experiences. The pros and cons, the ifs and buts, have been argued with stimulating vigor, and the next immediate objectives sketched out with both imagination and common sense. In every way these conferences, increasingly national and international in scope, have become pace-makers in the field of aging.

This Tenth Conference is, indeed, the most important of the whole series. Certainly, its topic "Free Time" offers us the greatest challenge of all. And it is quite in character that the University's Division of Gerontology, under Dr. Wilma Donahue, should be the first to devote an entire three-day session to exploring its significance.

When I speak of this matter of free or leisure time as offering the greatest challenge I mean this: in all the other areas that comprise the so-called aging problem we are at least dealing with something concrete. Granted that a vast amount of research and experiment is still needed, we nevertheless have working blueprints in the fields of health and rehabilitation, employment and economic security, housing, and community organization. Broadly speaking, we know what needs to be done and how to do it. What we require are the will and energy to carry through the effort.

The chapters which follow tell us that the abundance of free time represents a major revolution in human society and that it has enormous implications for health, for social roles, for community programs, for attitudes toward work; indeed, for the very place of work in our culture and for our entire value system. When we come to the question of how free time shall be used, however, there are no clear-cut outlines. We have the quickening sense that we are dealing with something that has no real shape or dimension. Yet, as the Tenth Conference has helped us to recognize, it constitutes the very heart of the whole matter of aging.

Recently, in an effort to gain a handhold somewhere, I made some rough calculations of the amount of leisure we have at our command. A century or so ago a man worked seventy hours a week and his average life expectancy was around forty years. Today, those figures are just reversed. Now, we have a forty-hour work week and a seventy-year life expectation. In other words, we have gained some 1,500 free hours each year. And this 1,500 hours multiplied by thirty (the increase in our life expectancy) comes to 45,000 hours, or twenty-two years of leisure added to our lives. For the housewife with simplified homemaking and with still longer life, the increment of leisure time is even greater.

This is what we have already achieved. It is not in the future. It is here now to be reckoned with. But stupendous as it seems, it is only the beginning. With the progress of automation, there is every likelihood that the work week will decline at an even more accelerated rate. When you couple this with steadily rising life expectancy, the impact on our society is almost incalculable. Thus it is that I believe the real core of our concern will always be how can we make the best use of this breath-taking gift of free time that has been vouchsafed us.

My own feeling is that this is one area in which we cannot hope to establish any overall blueprint. We are not dealing here with concrete objectives as in the other areas of our concern. We are dealing with the human spirit, and that is something quite different.

This is not to say, of course, that we cannot chart specific areas of the problem in which we are already at work. We can and are doing so. Certainly we should not discount the importance of the golden-age clubs which, as we all know, have mushroomed in such spectacular manner all over the country. Nor the growing number of activity centers with their well-organized programs. Nor the emphasis we place on creative activities in the arts and crafts and other kinds of creative effort. Nor the opportunities offered to make one-self more useful in community affairs.

All, or most of these, are to a certain extent subject to planning and execution. We are surely on the right track when we try our best to provide the facilities and the encouragement that will help our senior citizens and those approaching their later years make more effective use of their leisure time.

But this is only a part, a beginning, of the challenge we face. For no matter how we clothe our approach with fine phrases we cannot get away from the fact that, for the great majority of these older people, what we have to offer, or the activities or interests they seize upon, are at best, in their own minds at least, substitutes. Even with many of those who are thus most busily engaged, there is, I suspect, an inner feeling that they are filling a vacuum which has been created by this leisure time that has been thrust upon them.

In some way we must find the means of inculcating a more positive concept. In the past we have tended to look upon "time off" as time for recuperation and rest in order to return to work and produce more goods and services. Today, activity is urged upon older people as a means of preventing boredom and physical breakdown. Surely there must be greater rewards than the mere relief or prevention of distress.

The clear challenge is to discover and dramatize the value of leisure for its own sake.

We are all aware, of course, of the hurdles involved in such an undertaking. All human culture from time immemorial has been organized around work. The need to work in order to survive has shaped the very core of our attitudes and our institutions. The bulk of our population today has grown up in a work-a-day world oriented to job and family responsibilities. Retirement, when these responsibilities no longer exist, is simply a postscript.

This age has been called an age of materialism. It has also been called the age of anxiety. The two are not unrelated. The sickness of the age, if we may call it that, is the loss of any real meaning to our lives. Anyone who has dipped into current books on philosophy and religion knows how constantly this theme recurs. The fact that so many of us feel we have become merely cogs in a vast, all-encompassing industrial machine has made us lose sight of ourselves as individuals.

The answer to all this is to be found in the word recreation—recreation in its fundamental sense of *re-creation:* the opportunity to be born anew. There are plenty of people, we know, who are successfully negotiating the hazards of retirement and re-creating themselves, as individuals, in a gay, joyous, and exciting venture with some sort of creative activity. But for the great majority, their real concern is how to fill the vacuum.

This opportunity to re-create ourselves, to be born anew, must be grasped while we are still middle-aged. This is the period when our family responsibilities have been largely completed and the amount of free time increases rapidly.

Moreover, by this time, most of us have reached a plateau in our jobs or our professions. This is not to suggest that, for the specially qualified or the genuinely ambitious, there are not further peaks to be climbed. But for the generality of us, I think, we have probably attained the peak of job or career, and it is time to relax.

We can still do our day's work, honestly and competently. But we can also start thinking of our souls.

By thinking of our souls I am not speaking purely in a religious sense, though I would not for a moment discount the importance of that. I am thinking rather of a re-examination of ourselves as individuals and of our lives up to this point—to what extent we have found meaning and to what extent we have failed to find meaning, and then to realize quite soberly that this comparative leisure we have earned may stretch on for us for perhaps another quarter of a century.

How we are to make use of this gift of time is something that can be determined only by ourselves. There is no universal blueprint for it that is applicable to all. It cannot and should not be regimented. With a whole world of unexplored activities and interests at our command, we may be able to recapture some of the exhilaration we had as boys when we set off on our bicycles on a Saturday morning to see if we could discover what lay beyond the horizon.

It may take a generation, or more than a generation, before this concept begins to take root. But as it does we shall see a large and increasing segment of our population escaping the confines of our purely materialistic civilization. We shall have an army of men and women who, as individuals, are quietly recasting their values and reaching out for new meanings in life. In the process we, as a nation, shall be developing with these older people a store of wisdom in the truest sense of the word. This wisdom, in the aggregate, may well serve as a decisive ballast to the pressures and tensions of our age and as a means to diminish some of the anxieties that it has engendered.

Clark Tibbitts

June 26, 1957

Contents

FREE TIME

Challenge to Later Maturity

ROSALIE H. WAX, PH.D.

is an assistant professor of anthropology at the University of Chicago. Among her publications are "The Destruction of a Democratic Impulse" and "Reciprocity as a Field Technique." With her husband, Murray L. Wax, she co-authored "The Vikings and the Spirit of Capitalism."

Free Time in Other Cultures

All peoples give some meaning and order to the universe about them by categorizing the phenomena of life. Sometimes they establish their categories as polar opposites: a male principle versus a female principle, hot things versus cold, evil versus good; or the categories may simply note differences without opposing them to each other, e.g., broad flatness and long pointedness. Sometimes these categorizations are related to judgments of utility, superiority, or value, e.g., that masculine things are better than feminine.

We Americans distinguish between a mundane, practical, useful world of toil, a world in which every act is directed toward some preconceived goal, and its opposite, the world of free time, rest, and meditation. Moreover, we generally consider the world of work, or positive, teleological activity, to be the world of "real" value or significance. It keeps us alive and it is responsible for our "progress." In contrast, for many of us, the world of free time or play is unreal and undervalued. It requires activity that has no use, that is not directed toward any practical object or goal. We rest or play only when we "have nothing better to do."

Last year, I saw, in an excellent film of the almost extinct African Bushmen, an example of a people who did not seem to bother about distinguishing between work and play. In one scene a group of about nine or ten people were engaged in what we would call work. They were softening an animal skin so that it would be usable. All of the men, the old grandfather, the younger men, and the smallest boys sat in a circle and rhythmically massaged the skin. As they "worked," they recited an ancient chant led by the old man. When their women saw (and heard) this, they left what they had been doing and began to dance round and round the men. As I saw this, my hair stood on end, for the dancing women looked like certain rock paintings that were old before any man had built a house or sown seed.

I do not believe that any Bushman could tell us—or would be interested in telling us—which part of this activity was work and which was play. If we could enter the Bushman's mind and see this activity as he does, many of us would find the experience disturbing. Our mental comfort depends strongly on our system of categorization: to be comfortable with an activity we must define it as work or play. I venture to say you would be shocked if I were to deliver this paper while dancing the rock-and-roll, and you might fail to give it the serious consideration you now accord it.

Differences like this between the way we and the Bushmen would conceptualize free time and work make our task of discussing free time in other cultures both difficult and interesting. Other peoples not only have different attitudes toward free time and work than we do; they may not even distinguish between them in the same way we do. In examining other cultures, we have to be alternately narrow-minded and open-minded; we have to look doggedly for free time and yet accept the fact that the other culture may have a very different notion of free time from ours.

Let us begin with a people whose point of view is alien to ours, whose culture has been subjected to considerable study, and with whom we all have some familiarity: the wandering, buffalo-hunting warriors who once roamed our western plains.[1]

The fundamental life division made by the Plains Indians was not between work and nonwork, but between war and peace. For them, the world of war had to be kept out of contact with the world of peace. Thus, a warrior prepared himself to leave the peaceful world by elaborate ceremonials, and when he returned from the warpath he again changed himself by rituals so that he might re-enter the peaceful world. A warrior was supposed to be cruel and ferocious, he was allowed to boast, and he might be rude and proud, but the same man, as a man of peace, was supposed to be courteous, quiet-spoken, and intensely respectful of the wishes of others.

Interestingly, the most ferocious and successful warriors generally had little to say in the government of the community. This lay in the hands of the older men; more often than not, they had not been outstanding as warriors, but they were noted for their tact, skill in politics, and ability to compromise. Some tribes called such ideal peacetime leaders by a term meaning "a beloved old man."

The fundamental goal toward which every male strove was the acquisition of supernatural power. If he possessed

[1] I have drawn the greater part of this sketch from my husband's and my study of the Pawnee. However, the story of Old Woman's Grandchild comes from The Crow Indians by Robert H. Lowie (New York: Rinehart, 1956), pp. 144–45.

this power, all else would follow—he would be successful in hunting or warfare, and his fellows would regard him as a virtuous man. He obtained power by what I have called the Cinderella principle. That is, if a man were sufficiently humble and placed himself in a most pitiable, miserable, and helpless situation, the supernaturals would have compassion on him and grant him power.

The ideal Indian used such power to aid the members of his group. He led them on successful war parties or successful hunts. If he returned with booty—horses stolen from other tribes—one of his first acts was to give most of the horses away. If his power was so great that he still had much property in his possession, he gambled.

Whereas we gamble to free ourselves from the restraints of our sober, work-oriented lives and to obtain the thrill of participating in a slightly naughty and entirely impractical activity, the Indian gambled as a part of his "real" life and as an act of piety.

Anthropologists of an economic bent have pointed out that the Indian customs of exchanging gifts and gambling were economically utilitarian. The distribution of food and property was made more egalitarian and this strengthened the group. In addition, the distribution was practical for the giver, as well as the receiver. Most wealth consisted of horses, and one family could care for and use only a few. Since most horses had been stolen from the south and had difficulty with northern winters, the successful thief might just as well give them away and enjoy the reputation of generosity and virtue.

But I would like to point out that the practice of the giveaway and the practice of reckless gambling were both logically consistent with the Cinderella principle. The supernaturals had no interest in the rich and powerful man. By gambling recklessly, the pious Indian demonstrated his faith. If he won, the power was on him; he could gamble even more recklessly the next day or give his winnings away. If he lost everything, he put himself in the best possible situation for obtaining more power. For now, in his truly pitiable, poverty-stricken state, the supernaturals were bound to help him.

However we may look upon this kind of gambling, I do not think that we can accurately call it a free-time activity. And yet, all of the nineteenth-century observers were struck by the Indians' ability to take it easy. One of them, Mr. John T. Irving, Jr.,[2] tells us:

There is always an air of gentlemanly laziness hanging about Indians. They live they know not how, and they care not where. A little suffices them. If they can get it they are satisfied; if not, they are satisfied without it. . . . To all this is added a most gentlemanly abhorrence of labor of all descriptions, and a great store of patience in enduring the pinching hunger which is often the result of indolence. On a wet day you may travel for miles over the prairies . . . and not a single Indian will cross your path; but let the sun again beam forth, and you will see them around in every direction, lounging in the long grass or sunning themselves upon some high prairie peak, with a most profound forgetfulness of the past, and lordly contempt for the future . . .

In war or in hunting there is no being more untiring than the Indian. He will spend days and weeks in search of an enemy. Nothing is left undone to insure the successful accomplishment of his purpose. He endures fatigues of all kinds; fasting and peril are unheeded by him . . .

In peace, and in his own village, the Indian is a different being. He lounges about listlessly; he will sit for hours watching the children at their games; or he will stop at different lodges to hear the floating rumors of the town.

2 *Indian Sketches*, 1835, I, 23–25, 210.

Unfortunately, none of these observers asked the Indian how he felt during his relaxed and gentlemanly interludes. But perhaps we may hear the Indian himself speaking through one of his ancient folk tales. This is the story of Old Woman's Grandchild, a cultural hero who engaged in a contest with wicked supernatural snakes. The aim of the contest was to put the opponent to sleep by telling stories and then kill him.

The leader of the snakes began by saying: "In the spring the grass is green, in the shelter of young cherry trees the sun is a little warm, then when we lie down we feel like sleeping."

This pleasant picture might have put Old Woman's Grandchild to sleep. Fortunately, he possessed some magical arrows that kept him awake. When his turn came he said: "In the fall, whenever there is a little wind, when we lie in some shelter, when dried weeds rub against each other and we listen, we generally get drowsy, is it not so?" Only half the snakes answered "Yes." The rest were asleep. Old Woman's Grandchild continued: "In the daytime when it drizzles and the rain strikes the lodge pattering, we remain lying on the side, and warming our soles, then we fall asleep, is it not so? . . . At night, when we are about to lie down, listening to the wind rustling through the beech trees, we do not know how we get to sleep, but we fall asleep, is it not so?" This time no snake answered, but our hero made sure that all were helpless. "Having sought a hollow among the thickish pines, we make a fresh camp there. The wind blows on us, and we, rather tired, lie down and at the same time keep listening to the rustling pines until we fall asleep." When again no snake answered, Old Woman's Grandchild took out his knife and cut off their heads.

Neither the observations of the white man nor their own folk tales suggest that the Indian consciously divided his world into an area of work and an area of free time. He did, however, distinguish sharply between the sphere of war and the sphere of peace, and he alternated between periods of the most intense and concentrated predatory activity and an equally thorough relaxation. As far as I have been able to determine, he valued both his active and his placid moments (although young warriors sometimes sneered at the inactive older men and the older men tried to restrain the overambitious warriors). The tale of Old Woman's Grandchild suggests that the art of relaxation was highly developed and thoroughly enjoyed. It also suggests, however, that ferocious effort and relaxation could be curiously interwoven; for Old Woman's Grandchild fights his battle with the snakes not with warlike weapons but with hypnotic suggestions accessible only to an expert on sleep.

Let us now turn to the other side of the globe and look at another people—the Baluchi of western Pakistan.[3] These migratory people inhabit a very inhospitable environment. They live by sheepherding and, nominally, they are followers of Islam.

Their lives are divided into a sphere of duty or obligation necessary for life in civil society and an area which they call by a term which means the sphere of one's own will. They themselves seem to regard the latter as being one of freedom and distinct from the workaday world. But whereas we see the workaday world as the foundation of our existence, the Baluchi invert the emphasis. For them, the world

[3] All of the data cited comes from an unpublished manuscript prepared by Dr. and Mrs. Robert Pehrson, who, in 1954 and 1955, were the first anthropologists to study this remote group.

of their own will is the cherished area, the area in which they spend their energy and imagination and ingenuity.

The major "free-time" activity of the Baluchi is an ostensibly reckless and dangerous adultery. Theoretically, the penalty for adultery is death. But, the investigators assure us, if this penalty were rigidly enforced there would be very few Baluchi left alive. Apparently, it is enforced only enough to provide a spice of imminent danger and risk. A strict code of secrecy keeps many liaisons from discovery, and a reluctance to begin a blood feud prevents action on many of those that are discovered.

Baluchi economy and demography are peculiarly fitted to this particular free-time activity. The population is small and scattered, the men go off for long periods to watch their herds, and, by and large, everyone has a great deal of privacy. When their husbands are at home the women may still secretly play at the game, by embroidering skullcaps and tobacco pouches for their loves with silk thread brought to them by the objects of their affections.

A number of aspects of this complicated pastime resemble what Stephen Potter has called gamesmanship, that is: the art of winning without actually cheating.[4] These gamesmanlike attributes are not compatible with our ideal typical concept of play. Absolute or pure play, for us, requires only love of the game. It does not necessarily involve the spice of danger or naughtiness (though these phenomena manifest themselves in many of our free-time activities). Moreover, for us, absolute play is incorrigibly democratic. The essence of play is that anyone may play. In contrast, Baluchi adultery is markedly undemocratic. Influential men

[4] Stephen Potter, *The Theory and Practice of Gamesmanship* (New York: Henry Holt & Co., 1947).

or leaders are never punished or penalized. Young unmarried women may not participate. And finally, the game can offer no solace or entertainment to the aged.

Older people retire both from the political and economic responsibilities of the workaday world and from the game of adultery. Many devote themselves to piety and prayer. This piety, however, does not seem to be motivated by repentance for the misdeeds of youth. Rather, it is a resigned preparation for death.

In one respect the Baluchi point of view is easier for us to understand than is the view of the Plains Indians; for, like us, they distinguish between an area of sober, mundane, practical activity and an area of play or free will. But, as we have seen, they differ markedly from us in the emphasis they place on their world of play and in their picaresque insistence that one can only have fun and be really manly (or womanly) when one is doing what one ought not to do. This difference may not always have been so marked as it is today, for the medieval code of courtly love and the works of such authors as Rabelais and Alexandre Dumas bear witness that at least the aristocratic classes of Western society once placed a high value on reckless and romantic adultery.

Interestingly, at one point in its history one relatively sophisticated culture made so sharp and rigorous a distinction between work and sacred activities that a combination of the two was viewed as blasphemous. Here I refer to the rigorously enforced leisure of the pious medieval Jew, for when he was engaged in sacred matters, the Jew avoided anything remotely connected with work. He could not cook, light a lamp, carry any worldly object, or even take an extended walk. But though it was the polar opposite of practical, mundane activity, Judaic piety was by no means the same as play or free time. Indeed, it entailed more work and more trouble than any of the stringent, time-consuming activities of the secular world.

Even this very brief examination of a number of cultures has shown us that some people do not order their lives by setting up a distinction between free time and work time. The fact that they are not interested in such a categorization does not mean, however, that they do not possess a great deal of what we would call "free time" and that they do not employ this time enjoyably. Thus, the Indian grandfather who sat and watched the children play might not have been aware that he was loafing, but I strongly suspect that he enjoyed himself. Again, the tale of Old Woman's Grandchild and the snake people reflects a marked development in the art of living. Any people who can think of so many delightful ways of falling asleep are experts in the use of free time—whether they consciously know this or not.

In our discussion of the Plains Indians, we observed that an activity, like gambling, which has for us no proper connection with work or the mundane world, was, for the Indian, an integral and important part of his serious and sacred world. Consciously, when the Indian gambled or recklessly gave away his property he showed his trust in the supernatural goings. Unconsciously, he kept his economy functioning.

Then, when we considered the Baluchi and, very briefly, the medieval Jews, we observed that both resemble us in making a fairly clear distinction between work time and free time. But both of them differ from us in that we tend to consider free time as "a residue sphere left over from work-time," [5] whereas, for the Baluchi and the Jew, work time might almost be called a residue left over from the demands of the more important or more interesting sphere of nonwork. Or, at least, we may say that for these peoples the sphere of nonwork is (or was) more significant and satisfying than the sphere of work.

Although the Baluchi and the Jew define nonwork as the more salient part of life, they have very different conceptions of what one ought to do in one's free time. The Baluchi is a gamesman and devotes his creative energies to being attractively wicked. The Jew, on the other hand, defined the sphere of nonwork as supremely sacred. Undoubtedly, he derived a sober pleasure from his pious, utterly nonmundane activities, but we cannot say that he used his strangely unfree time for fun. Perhaps to really have fun one must be a little naughty.

We cannot solve our particular problem of free time by adopting or imitating the particular practices of other cultures. This does not mean that we are worse off than those with the cultures that tend to blur the distinction between work and play or that value them differently than we do. They, too, have their problems.

The Plains Indians, we have seen, divided their world between a sphere of active predation and serene placidity and had to cope with rebellious young men who wished to extend the first sphere into the second. The Baluchi, it appears, have put themselves into a situation in which they have to be naughty or immoral in order to be free. The more sophisticated medieval Jew, who defined work as the opposite

[5] David Riesman, *The Lonely Crowd* (New York: Doubleday & Co., 1953), p. 315.

of sacredness but lived in a world in which he had to work, found himself in a situation of extraordinary tension.

We, who came very close to defining practical, goal-oriented work as sacred, now find ourselves with an ever-increasing amount of time on our hands. Nevertheless, in this process, we may have forged a tool which may help us solve our problem. For while we were trying to associate the former with most of the virtuous and moral qualities of our society, we have unwittingly defined play as an activity in which these virtues receive their ultimate or ideal expression. By this paradoxical statement I mean that while we may think that we are free and democratic in our workaday lives, most of us are capable of being genuinely free and democratic only when we play.

We define play in terms of freedom: as an activity which we undertake only for the joy of doing it and only for its own sake. Though we follow rules when we play, we accept these rules not because they are useful or virtuous, but because we choose to follow them.

The democracy inherent in genuine civilized play is one of its most wonderful and unappreciated aspects; for when we are real chess-players, expert fishermen, or skilled conversationalists, the age, status, profession, or sex of our coparticipants become a matter of no significance. We can "play" with a child, an old lady, a juvenile delinquent, a professor, a plumber, or a man from Mars, and what matters is not their rank, race, or status, but whether they can play the game. I have been most deeply impressed by this phenomenon while fishing in Chicago's Jackson Park lagoon. Most of my cofishermen are Negroes, old ladies, children, men of all ages. And here I felt that we treated one another as if we were real persons.

The unsophisticated or primitive peoples do not, so far as I know, participate in this kind of deliberate, consciously impractical, and extraordinarily democratic kind of free-time activity. Often, when they play they do not know that they play. When they see themselves as playing they tend to be excessively ceremonious and formal. And, as we saw in the case of the Baluchi, their "play" may not be particularly democratic.

While I know very little about this, my guess is that many of the unsophisticated peoples really do not need an elaborate definition of play—and that we, in our culture, need it very much. First of all, the primitive peoples usually do not emphasize work or pursue mundane ends to the degree that we do. Without being formal or self-conscious about it, they approach a great many of their daily activities as if they were play. Secondly, the primitive people usually do not have the elaborate rank and status differentiations that we possess. In consequence, they can communicate with each other much more easily on a fundamental human level. And finally, most primitive peoples experience a deep and emphatic sense of similarity or likeness to other members of their group. They know they are one and the same. But we, when we work, are forced to maintain subtle differences between ourselves and our inferiors and superiors and, at the same time, are forced to be intimate or friendly with all sorts of people, merely because they happen to be our colleagues, our co-workers, or because we happen to belong to the same age group. Only when we play can we escape from both this enforced separation and this enforced intimacy and experience the profound kinship of an unfettered, unthreatening community of interest.

Many observers of modern society are depressed by

the possibility that our conception of play may be still further invaded and perverted by the powerful unfree areas of our culture. This happened in the last century, and it is happening in a different manner today. Most of you are aware that our holidays, especially Christmas, now entail more work than fun. Even more insidious is the increasing tendency to force everyone to "join in the fun," to take up certain "free-time" activities not for their own sake but because everyone else is doing them, or because the people in the circle we wish to enter are doing them.

I cannot bring myself to share this pessimistic outlook. We know little about play or about the idea of free time. What we do know suggests that the forces that support it are as insidious and powerful as those which support work. We, like most mammals, are born with a marked predisposition to learn to play. We are not born with a similar disposition to work—at least according to the definition we have constructed for ourselves. Again, the insidious nature of play and our hidden affection for it may be illustrated by the fact that, though we have tried to rob it of value and significance, we have covertly related it to some of our most treasured ideals, the ideal of freedom and the ideal of democracy.

CLARK TIBBITTS
is assistant director, Special Staff on Aging of the
U. S. Department of Health, Education, and Welfare
in Washington, D.C. He was formerly director of the
Institute for Human Adjustment, Horace H. Rack-
ham School of Graduate Studies, University of
Michigan. His publications include numerous articles
on medical economics, human adjustment, and aging.

Aging as a Modern Social Achievement *

We all know that the world constantly
changes, but not all of us recognize that the rate of change
has speeded up tremendously in recent times. In his book
Utopia, 1976 Morris Ernst makes the statement that American society has gone through more changes since the nation
was founded than occurred in the preceding million years
of man's existence. One of the changes, the one to which we
will give our attention in this paper, is the remarkable increase in the number of middle-aged and older people in
the population. Man's ancient desire to live longer and better
is being realized at last.

Average life expectancy at birth has increased by 75
per cent over the past century, and each new advance is

* Reprinted from "Aging in the Modern World," a study discussion series developed by the Division of Gerontology, University of
Michigan, with the financial assistance of The Fund for Adult Education. This material was presented on the conference program in the
form of a film entitled "Aging—Modern Social Achievement," which
was developed under the same auspices.

hailed as a triumph of modern medical science. Simultaneously, the problems of adjustment to longer life, described historically by Professor Simmons in his discussion of aging in other cultures, have been multiplied, and new ones are constantly being added. This is because more people are living longer in a society which is itself constantly becoming more complex. The growing number of old people challenges us to find satisfactory solutions to problems of health, family relations, housing, employment, income security, and use of free time. These problems are occupying the attention of more and more students and researchers, political leaders, the staffs of public and private agencies, and even entire communities and states. If all this energy expended on their behalf is not to fail of its purpose, older people themselves must co-operate in full measure. Older persons will not achieve satisfaction in their lives if they are but passive objects of the benevolence of experts and specialists.

The presence in the population of nearly 50 million persons beyond the age of forty-five years who are reasonably certain of a good many years of free time in the future is an unprecedented social achievement. Indeed, aging may best be defined as the survival of a growing number of people who have completed the traditional adult roles of making a living and child-rearing. The years after the completion of these tasks are beginning to represent an extension of life marked by a shortening of hours of work, both on the job and in the home and, in the end, complete retirement from paid employment. In short, the extension of life has brought into being a new turning point in life that needs sharper recognition by more and more people.

If people who reach this point are wise they will find fulfillment in life by utilizing their leisure for new and different activities designed to give them new satisfactions. But there is more than a suspicion, unhappily, that many fail to recognize this and, instead, occupy their leisure with mere "busywork" that yields little worth-while return and that others, even more unfortunate, are overtaken by boredom and dissatisfaction.

More years of life for all! Time for enriched living? Or time for boredom? What, really, is the origin of this remarkable situation with its challenging dilemma? How has this longer life, with its promise of increased leisure, been achieved? Is it real or merely a figment of the specialist's imagination? What, actually, does it mean for an individual person? For society at large? Can it be afforded—by society, by the individual? What is the future of this situation, and what are the answers to the questions it poses?

Some of the answers are at hand, particularly those having to do with the genesis of the situation. But the proper utilization of the opportunities opened to those who actually achieve the longer life we are talking about is a wide-open question, both in its personal and social aspects. We are going to discuss both aspects of the matter, but on this particular occasion we are going to take a look at some of the underlying factors: the revolutionary changes taking place in our culture.

Aging: Fostered by Scientific and Technological Development

Longer, healthier, and easier living is a direct outgrowth of the application of science to achieve better nutrition, medical care, and conditions of living; and to develop new forms of energy and new machines to do our work. Before this happened—before the systematic use of science became a marked characteristic of our society—the task of making a living and the carrying out of household duties occupied everybody throughout relatively short lives. This pattern of working and living persisted as normal for society for many decades of our own country's history, as Professor Simmons has shown. Gradually the introduction of new tools and machines, the use of water power and steam, and improved understanding of nutrition and medicine began to create new patterns of living and to lengthen life. But only during the last fifty years or so has the full impact of the change been felt by everybody in this country.

More People, More Years

Since 1900 the number of persons beyond the age of forty-five has increased from 13 million then, to 47 million today, or to about as many people as were living in the United States in 1880. Today also there are actually more people over sixty-five than there were people of all ages in this country in 1830.

Partly this is accounted for by the fact that there are more people. The total population has grown from 23 million in 1850 to 166 million today. This increase, including larger numbers of people in all the age brackets, accounts for about half the increase in the number of older people since 1900.

A second influential factor at work here is immigration. During the last century and through the first decade of the present century, millions of people sought a new life in America. Coming largely as youths and young adults, the immigrants eventually became part of the middle-aged and older groups. They account for about 20 per cent of the total increase in the upper ages since 1900.

The third factor is the improvement of the environment in terms of health: techniques for purifying milk and water were introduced, the sanitary handling of waste was mastered, vital advances in nutrition through modifications of eating habits were made, the infectious diseases of infancy, childhood, and, increasingly, adulthood were brought under control. As a consequence, more children are living into early adulthood, and more adults into their middle and later years. Life expectancy at birth has increased from about forty years in 1850, to about forty-nine years in 1900, and to seventy years today. The life expectancy of those who reach the age of forty has increased less dramatically, but still it has moved from about twenty-eight more years to thirty-four more years over the century and is expected to continue to rise.

America's aging citizenry, then, is in large part the product of population growth, immigration, medical progress, and improved environmental conditions. Since all the causes, except large-scale immigration, continue to operate, it may be predicted that around the year 2000 the population will have increased to 275 to 300 million, with from 80 to 85 million persons aged forty-five years and over, of whom perhaps 25 million will be over three-score-and-ten. Millions now living are practically certain to live into the years assumed to be the proper years for retirement.

Patterns of Making a Living Have Changed

The way of living has also changed spectacularly. In the earlier decades of this country's history, most work was done on the home farm and in so-called cottage industries, with simple tools operated by hand or powered by animal energy. The output of each worker was relatively small— little more than enough to provide subsistence for his own family. Children normally went to work at eight or ten years of age, and most people continued to work as long as they lived. Millions were worn out by forty-five or fifty. Many died "before their time," as the expression was, and only a few lived into old age. This was the general picture.

But man was not satisfied with this hard, frugal, and short life. He strove for a higher standard of living attained with less work, and the principal means to his end was the machine. New sources of energy were brought into use: water, steam, electricity. Technological change became an outstanding characteristic of our society.

The speed of change was remarkable. In 1850 the total amount of energy produced and expended in making a living is estimated to have been 10 billion horsepower-hours, or 440 horsepower-hours for each person in the population. Around two-thirds of this was supplied by human and animal muscles. By 1950 the amount of energy used had increased to nearly 700 billion horsepower-hours, 98 per cent of it from inanimate sources. Today every man, woman, and child in this country commands the equivalent of 4,500 horsepower-hours of work each year, more than tenfold increase in but four generations.

At first the increases in output were small. People worked long hours at their machines to produce as much as they could. By 1900, however, people began to extract other advantages from the machine. They decided to "take out" a proportion of the results in shorter hours of work. The work week began to shorten. It shortened at the rate of about three hours every ten years. At the same time it became possible to keep children off the labor market and in school longer. And, at the other end of life, more people began to find it possible to drop out of the labor force and enjoy a few years of leisure. By 1900 about 35 per cent of the older men were retired, most of them because they were physically unable to go on working in full-time competitive employment; but some had retired because they had been able to harvest the fruits of machine productivity in leisure.

It is since 1900 that the latter group, our concern here, has grown at a tremendous pace. The length of the work week has now dropped below forty hours for many; the average age of entry into gainful employment or paid work has risen to eighteen or nineteen; and more and more people are able drastically to reduce their hours of work or to quit altogether. Today 14 per cent of all men between forty-five and sixty-four, 60 per cent of those sixty-five and over, and 80 per cent of those over seventy-five are not in paid employment. The proportions of older women not gainfully employed are much greater.

This remarkable change in the pattern of people's work histories—later entry into paid employment, earlier withdrawal from it—has occurred at a time when the level of living in this country has been rising. Twice as much in goods and services for each person in our population of 166 million is now produced as was produced per person for the 76 million of 1900. The level of living has greatly improved, and, while prices have increased tremendously, so have wages. Real income—or the quantity of goods and services you can buy with your money income—has sharply increased. All this tends to prove the point that our society can afford the leisure it is granting its older citizens. If we continue along present lines into the future, more and more people will have the leisure we are talking about.

We are, in short, only at the beginning of this development. New varieties of energy and new kinds of machines are now coming into use. Power from atoms, energy from the sun are being harnessed. Automation or the skillful co-ordination of machines is a living actuality. Output seems bound to increase, the standard work week to continue to shorten. It is rather confidently predicted that by 1965 the work week will be down another three or four hours and will probably reach thirty hours by 1975. Real income will go up 20 per cent or more. Per capita purchasing power in 2000 will be double what it is now. And more people will look forward to retirement as a normal phase of the cycle of life, just as they will accept prolonged educational preparation for the earlier phases of the life cycle.

Disappearance of the Household and Its Economy

Science, technology, and factories have profoundly affected family living. In agricultural-handicraft societies the household is the unit of production, not the factory, the office, or the large store. The chief breadwinner in such societies works at or very near his home, assisted actively by his wife, children, and such relatives as are living with him. Most food and clothing are produced at home, and "exotic" foods like sugar, tea, and coffee are obtained by selling the small surplus of home-produced goods as are decorative clothing and household objects.

In such households most of the children were trained for their occupations in the household, primarily with the idea of carrying the pattern of life forward into the future. The sick were cared for at home. Even religious life was integrated into the family routine by grace before meals and Bible reading and prayers at the close of the day. The cultural life of adults—who may or may not have had a maximum of four years at school—was what they made it through reading newspapers and farm magazines. Recreation was created at home, even if in association with neighbors. As the seniors got older, they continued to work but slowly shifted to lighter tasks. The traditional final place for the very old was the chimney corner. One can get pleasurably nostalgic about all this, but as a way of life it has vanished forever for most Americans.

It has vanished as the country has industrialized and urbanized. Factories and cities have killed it. Today the head of the family, and often his wife also, works outside the home. Food and clothing are now purchased ready for use. Most educational and religious activities are carried on wholly in outside community institutions. Even recreation has, in large measure, to be sought outside the home. Only occasionally is sickness taken care of within the home; the more usual practice is to send the sick to hospitals. Houses have shrunk in size, and they are streamlined. The work in them is done as far as possible by machines: washers, vacuum cleaners, toasters, mixers, et cetera.

The gist of it is that the so-called economic-kinship household of our ancestors has dissolved into its component parts. Young married people, with or without children, with the aid of mass-produced and mass-distributed goods and services, have achieved a new kind of self-sufficiency, a localized self-sufficiency. They find little need for the help of additional persons permanently resident in the home and often get along employing only a baby sitter occasionally. There is no room for others, really. Each generation related to this new family unit tends to develop its associations with others of similar age *outside the home*. The generations tend to lead lives of their own from a relatively early age, assuming that their elders will do likewise—and continue to do so throughout their lives. The closely knit household of kinship groups of various ages is not provided for in the new scheme of society. This new way of life is a natural consequence of modern, industrial civilization. This is what we in large measure face today. It practically forces the older people to "make their own lives."

And this bids fair to continue indefinitely into the future. True, the population is growing rapidly, and the number of families has doubled in the last generation; but almost all the new families are modeled on this new pattern just described.

Age as Opportunity

In our society the adult years have been lengthened and may now be divided into more or less distinct phases; or, perhaps better, an entirely new period has been added to life.

Early adulthood can be described as the period from twenty to twenty-five up to forty or fifty, during which the individual is occupied with creating a family, establishing a place in the community, fixing upon a career, and striving for advancement. Interest is largely focused on immediate individual needs and the family.

Middle life, or the years from forty or forty-five to fifty-five or sixty, brings many changes and is coming to be recognized as a period of transition from early to mature adulthood. Most persons are by this time well established in career occupations. Children, by and large, are now on their own, so that the pressures and responsibilities of parenthood are mainly over. Many persons at this period of life begin to realize that they have more time for the interests they were forced to set aside in early adulthood, or for entirely new interests. And most adults at this time begin to look forward to retirement.

This remarkable innovation in the life pattern has been made possible by the amazing advances in science, leading to longer life and unprecedented productivity. Middle life is the time when a person finds himself completing one role in life and looking for a new one. It is the stage at which opportunity for new adventures in personal growth arises and the exploration of new interests becomes possible, after long years of hard work and heavy family responsibilities.

Can the Good Life Be Found?

This situation demands careful appraisal. What is being done? Are people enjoying it? Are they using their energy and free time in ways that are satisfying? Where are they to look for new growth and adventure? What are the essential conditions of a really satisfying later life?

These are new and important questions. They are questions that must be answered constructively. There is little precedent to guide the individual. Expectations and duties for the earlier years are fully defined by a long tradition. There are few real choices to be made in childhood or in the early adult years. A man knows fairly well what is expected of him. But this is not true of the new phase of life we are talking about. There are few guidelines, because no society has ever before known the mass extension of life and leisure that is now upon us. Both individuals and society are embarked on uncharted seas, on a new phase of life activity, with little accumulated understanding of it.

Many people are finding their way to rich adventure. They are the path makers to the future. They have assessed themselves, examined their situations, potentialities, and interests, and have made their choices. Some intensify their contributions to community activities, some turn to educational activities to clarify and amplify their understanding of the life of mankind and themselves, some seek to sharpen their perceptions in the arts by cultivating an interest in literature, painting, and music. Some seek to express themselves in the arts or in crafts. Some turn to a mixture of these things and further spice it up by travel. Or they stay at home and use their talents to make it a more beautiful place than ever it was before.

Whatever they do, they are explorers, pioneers. They are the pioneers of the new "prime of life" that has been vouchsafed to so many Americans by medicine and technology. What will their explorations mean for their fellows and society at large? Are they on the way toward adding not only a new dimension to their own lives but also a new dimension to civilization in the United States of America?

JOHN E. ANDERSON, PH.D.

is a professor of psychology and former director of the
Institute of Child Welfare at the University of Min-
nesota. He is the author of numerous articles and
books on experimental, animal, and development
psychology.

Psychological Aspects
of the Use of Free Time

The problem I am to discuss is of particular
interest because of the great shift in our point of view with
regard to older people. There was a time when older people
were supposed to work; that is, to continue productive
activity until they were physically unable to do so. This
is still the pattern in many societies, even though certain old
people may be freed from the standard. But in our society
and in most Occidental countries the concept of retirement
has so entered into the picture that we expect people to cease
productive work at sixty, sixty-five, or seventy. This means
a transition from the work- and money-oriented value system
of an older society to a free-time program with living costs
met.

This reformation in society's view of older people has
been going on for half a century and particularly in the last
twenty-five years. It is legally recognized in our social
security programs, in income tax legislation, and in various
pension, insurance, and retirement plans, all of which set
a definite age limit for benefits. Very large segments of our

population expect to cease productive activity at a definite age and thereafter enjoy the hypothetical comforts and peace that go with release from the worries attendant upon working in our social order.

Much attention, of course, has gone to the legal and financial aspects of retirement; and various devices such as pre- and post-retirement counseling have been developed for cushioning the transition. But I am concerned with certain psychological principles that underlie the system of relations that are concerned with the use of free time in the hope that the nature of the program that might aid older persons in effective adjustment to the change in status may become clear.

These questions deserve serious consideration, since we expect the person to move from a work-oriented and money-oriented program of full-time activity to a program in which he will determine his own activities and thus become creative until death. For most people this puts the emphasis upon a type of behavior with which they have not been concerned since early childhood.

Involved in some degree is the increasing longevity of our population which means not only a larger and larger number of persons both relatively and absolutely in this status, but also that more are included for a longer time.

In this paper I am interested mainly in the person between sixty-five and seventy-five. Two other groups of age-related problems arise. One concerns the person between forty-five and sixty-five, and arises out of our pension and security plans that create unemployment problems at this age level not easily solved. The other group covers the people who reach the age of seventy-five or eighty years and who need custodial or bed care. These are the very old people for whom special care is necessary. This is, however, one misconception which should be clarified.

Many think of the problem of the activity of older persons in terms of residence in Florida or California; we have the myth of leaving the home community and going off to a very pleasant and idyllic place to live. But when we look at the facts about older people we find that those who move make up a very small proportion of the total, and, of those who go, many return to their former communities. This means that, first, the problems of older persons are ones of the local community and state rather than ones of an idyllic place far away. Second, people who move carry their personal needs with them and face precisely the same problems of time-filling, engaging activities wherever they go. Wherever and whenever we find older people, they are concerned in some degree with this problem.

A Preliminary Analysis of the Organization of Energy

Our discussion may well begin a preliminary analysis of the organization of energy or the development of time-filling activities throughout the life span. If we look at the total picture we see that the young child is a very active, energetic creature who is always looking for outlets for his energy. He does many different things in a somewhat random fashion during most of his waking period. He responds both to his needs and to the external objects that attract him. Over a period of years he gradually works out a schedule of activities in which specific times are allotted for particular activities. Although much of this organization is imposed by the demands of his environment, that is, the training of parents and teachers, there is evidence that apart from such demands the

person routinizes or schedules his physiological and psychological activities. Even young babies work out eating schedules that are quite constant. As time passes, more and more
the life is patterned whether the demand arises internally or
under social pressure.

In one sense the life of the infant is multipotential in that
there is an almost unlimited range of activities that might be
developed. Studies of children show them engaged in a wide
variety of different activities in the course of their exploration of themselves and of the possibilities of the environment.
But gradually specific things come to be done at specific
times in response to the social demands. Finally there results
a person with most of his time occupied.

Selection of Activities

One other feature of this process might also be mentioned, namely, the selection which goes on. From the broad
base of many activities with which concern is brief and somewhat superficial, the person moves to a few major activities
with which concern is deep. In this process it has been said
that efficiency is purchased at the cost of versatility. There
also comes a highly differentiated series of roles or compart-
ments into which life's activities are fitted.

Distinction between Work and Leisure Activities

The result or outcome of this development is a sharp
distinction between work and what are ordinarily called leisure activities. Work is an activity that is done under conditions in which there are demands with respect to time and
place and in which goods or services are produced which can

be exchanged for the goods or services of other persons. The adult, whether man or woman, devotes a major part of his time with fair regularity to what we call production either by himself or in company with his fellows. Years ago almost all of the daylight hours were spent in production because a living was hard to come by. But in our society with its high rate of production the individual typically works, say, forty hours a week, and produces and spends the remainder of his time in personal, social, family, and recreational matters. Where formerly there were infrequent rest periods or vacations, now there are in addition a substantial number of hours each week devoted to recreation.

In leisure-time activities, theoretically at least, the demands are self-imposed; there is some feeling of freedom and there is a sharp contrast to the external controls of time, space, and production imposed in the work situation.

It is true that in every society there are a few persons of a very creative type who impose their own controls because of the quality of their production. We are not speaking about this small group of creative individuals who sell unusual services or products that are in great demand by society, but rather about the mass of persons who must meet demands of time and place.

Sometimes we think of such recreational activity as essentially play and we make a contrast between work and play. But this contrast is not so helpful as it seems on first glance. Many of the modern students of children look upon their play as essentially their work in that the child's play is made up of time-filling activities in which he is developing his perception, acquiring skill and knowledge, and participating in social relations—all of which contribute directly to organizing behavior. A surprising proportion of all the child's responses come later to have utility. A child's play is not recreation but a business, whereas the adult's play is generally not a business but a recreation.

Superimposed upon this business of the child finding himself, there are imposed the work requirements of society that utilize the skills the child has developed by channeling them directly. When the child reaches six, society places him in school and proceeds over a number of years in a formally organized endeavor to channel the child's capacities. At the same time it is training him in ways to expend his energies by making demands of time, place, and production. The school becomes identified with work and comes to possess more and more of the characteristics of work. As time passes recreation, rest, and leisure become more sharply differentiated.

The retired person is then returned to the status which corresponds to that of the child, in that he has time on his hands without the social demands that characterize the work situation. He has to change the attitudes that have been built up in a lifetime of working and to proceed to reorganize his life. He may well find that the hobby that gave him rest and recreation when pursued as a major activity no longer holds him because it fails to possess the characteristics that work possesses. With this point we shall be more concerned later.

Before considering some of the implications of this view let us consider some of the facts brought out in the Friedmann and Havighurst studies in *The Meaning of Work and Retirement*. Their studies illustrate some of the basic principles in considering the adjustment pattern. They interviewed many people from many occupations before and after retirement and studied their ways of meeting the transition.

Adjustment of Men and Women to Retirement

One result was striking, namely, the time it takes for the person to adjust. The man of sixty-five faces the same problem that the married woman faces fifteen or twenty years earlier when she finds her children gone and her household restricted to her husband and herself. The care of the home is now simple because the children, who have been the real center of interest, are gone, so that she needs to change her role and to develop engaging activities to fill her time. As the family patterns change, a change of role becomes inevitable. Many women develop interests in community, philanthropic, religious, or social activities. In fact, a large proportion of the voluntary programs in our modern society are carried on by women who have made this transition.

For the man the work situation fulfills much the same purpose as does the family for the woman. In the interviews of older men about their former work, it appeared that dominant in the minds of many of the men were the social contacts afforded by the work itself rather than what was done. These men missed the gang, the office group, the team, the organization to which they had devoted so much of their lives. Part of the problem of readjustment involved filling the gap in social relations or, more specifically, the day-to-day or hour-by-hour contact with other persons provided by the work situation. This is an interesting finding because most of us do not usually think of work as an area about which substantial group and social relations are built.

Next, the man had to find ways of filling the large amount of time he had on his hands. True, the first six weeks or two months passed quickly and were rather like a vacation. Then time weighed heavily because the holding power of temporary leisure time and recreational activities to which he had looked forward was gone.

Wives made the transition of their husbands to retirement without much difficulty because they continued with the same tasks, interests, and social contacts with friends and neighbors they had held previous to retirement. The retired single working woman when compared with men in comparable work areas showed adjustment patterns like those of working men. The single woman was lost, needed to reorganize her life, sought time-filling activities.

There is also a marked relation to earlier experience. When retired steelworkers in the city were compared with retired coal miners in southern Illinois radical differences in adjustment were found. The city steelworker had almost no resources. It took him some months to work out a schedule in which he wandered about the city for a while, watched a construction job in process, dropped into the barbershop to read the newspaper, went somewhere else for a short time, then turned up in another place, and finally returned home. It is of some interest that over a period of time these patterns become consistent and that thereafter much the same routine was followed day after day and that with the appearance of a stable daily schedule, emotional and personal problems tended to disappear. Building a personal schedule of time-filling activities took from six months to a year and was very difficult for the city worker.

The coal miners, on the other hand, who had lived all their lives in rural or semirural areas on three- to five-acre plots on which they had a cow, a few chickens, a garden, and perhaps an acre or two in some crop made the transition easily and effectively because they increased their activities on the land and did not have to work out completely new schedules.

In general the higher the educational level of the person the better he met retirement, because he had a larger repertoire of skills and of interests and thus had more varied activities to which to turn.

Self-employed persons, particularly doctors, lawyers, small businessmen, and so on made the transition with relative ease because they literally almost never retired. They kept some type of activity going which was in line with their earlier experience and vocation, and they did not therefore experience a very sharp break. Farmers too are people who do not characteristically retire. They keep up some kind of farming activity, often on a small plot of land near a neighboring town. When retiring farmers make a very sharp break by moving into a city or into a radically different community they do not seem to adjust as well.

For salaried persons and wage earners there is a sharp cutoff which is clearly defined. One day the worker is fully employed; the next he has nothing to do. The people who are affected are those in major industries, in many types of business, in public service, in governmental service, in fact in every occupation with a fixed retirement age.

This group of studies interested me very much because they seemed to bring to the fore a major problem in adjustment to aging that has not received much discussion. In much of our thinking and talking about activities for older persons we consider relatively short-time interests and activities. We think of recreation and entertainment. But if we look at the meaning of the work pattern in the life of the person, we see that it not only bulks very large from the standpoint of time but also from the standpoint of social relationships and continuing interest patterns. When we ask how the activities we propose for older people measure up to the model provided by work, deficiencies in our thinking appear.

Let us then examine work in terms of its psychological characteristics quite apart from its demands of time and place. We notice that first of all it is a productive activity that has a value to society which is recognized by the self and by others. Leisure activities sometimes have this characteristic but more often do not. Second, it is a way of acting which has developed over many years and to which various interests and values have accrued. Third, it has a certain degree of complexity which holds the person. Even in very monotonous activities there are variations and relations which enter and make persistent production possible. Fourth, it is a continuing activity with which the person identifies and interacts. Fifth, as has already been brought out, it is a nexus of social relations.

Contrast these features of work with the characteristics of the ordinary activities with which we in adult life associate patterns of leisure and entertainment and you will find that in much of our thinking emphasis goes to entertainment and momentary activities, which from the psychological point of view are mainly situational and transactional. These are carried on largely for the pleasure they give at the moment. There are, however, recreational activities such as hobbies which achieve some degree of organization in time and to which the person turns from time to time. They occupy a somewhat intermediate position between entertainment and work. Work can then be considered as an activity that possesses complexity and the possibility of continuing relations that give it interest and zest.

Years ago in research on the diversion of young children by interrupting their activities, some rather interesting things were discovered about the nature of the task that pulls a child away from other activities. Generally speaking the more complex the activity from which you are trying to pull the child the more necessary it is to use a diverting activity of about the same complexity. In other words a simple activity will not divert a person away from a complex activity or break up an interest pattern. This is, to my mind, an important aspect of an activity, since it indicates that a good activity for persons—except when we consider pure entertainment—relates in some sense to the degree to which it offers an opportunity for the person to reveal his own resources. Involved in complexity is a change in the task itself from time to time and the factor that in the course of such changes the person will be permitted to move on to more advanced levels of performance and more interesting aspects of the task.

In other words we are talking about a type of interaction between the person and the task in which the task brings out the person's resources and in so doing permits the person to feel that he is growing or developing. In the studies of hobbies it is found that people put into their hobby the complexities that make it possible to maintain such continued interest. Thus the stamp collector becomes interested in perforations and minor modifications, the collector of old glass in peculiar minor variations that he can identify. Children going about their spontaneous activities elaborate and refine them and thus increase the complexity of the performance. Thus hopscotch or bounce the ball becomes elaborated into complex rigmaroles.

Obviously these characteristics exist in different human

activities and jobs in various degrees. Obviously also there is wide variation in persons. Some are satisfied and happy with limited participation and simple repetitive activities while others demand high complexity and much progressive change. What I am concerned with, however, is not so much these individual variations as how we can design activities that will occupy older persons over substantial periods of time and will give them the same type of personal results as do the work activities which they have left.

This brings us to the concept of a work substitute as a device that comes close to the heart of the matter. There is far too great a tendency to think of the activities of older people in terms of leisure, recreational, or entertainment activities which are done for momentary rest or as a relief from other activities. Too little attention is given to thinking of activities that will do over a period of years what work did at an earlier period. From what we have already said, we can describe some of the characteristics of the ideal kind of activity to meet the need. One characteristic, first of all, is a substantial degree of continuity in time so that the individual can return to the activity again and again and can identify himself with it as a significant and essential part of his being. For him to do this, the activity must be complex. One of my friends who retired volunteered for hospital work and was set at the job of folding bandages. She was a bright and clever woman. After several weeks, however, she became so bored with folding bandages that she had to stop, even though she was looking for a time-filling activity.

When we examine the activities we propose for older persons from this point of view, we find that many of our programs are deficient because they are conceived in terms of short-time activities, in terms of entertainment rather than education, in terms of superficial concern rather than real devotion. Let us examine our proposals in terms of their holding power and the extent to which older persons can become interested in them over time. Let us think of work substitutes that will do psychologically for the person what work does for him in his period of maturity.

Sometimes it is said that the person at younger age levels should develop major secondary activities with which he can be concerned after he retires and which will come to function as work substitutes. I am not quite sure, however, that this principle will always operate, even though it happens sometimes. Some persons develop an extreme interest and become very much concerned in a secondary activity and use retirement as an opportunity to plunge into the activity full speed. But for many persons, such a secondary activity is a recreational or restful activity which, in the framework of the work situation, has a very specific function. As soon as you remove the work the secondary activity loses its interest because it no longer has a real function.

This suggests that in order to build an effective program at older age levels we must build it as a new product, even though it is based on past interests and activities.

We may well consider searching the various activities which are proposed for older persons in terms of a conceptual framework of this type and seek out activities and programs that will do the job. Obviously, we must not be afraid of long-time, complex, and difficult pursuits.

Another thought which occurs to me is that from the standpoint of the individual's mental health, such an engaging activity, regardless of whether it contributes to society or not, may be quite desirable. I am asking what an activity does for the individual—not whether or not it is socially useful.

But it does seem to me that in addition to considering the value of the activity to the person, it is desirable from the social point of view to fully use the resources of the person rather than to fritter them away. If we can develop complex, time-holding activities that contribute to society in which persons can become deeply concerned, all the better. How we can fit them into our work- and money-oriented society is another problem.

For a moment I should like to couple the concept of activities of deep concern with that of self-help. We have moved from a period in which we thought of older persons very largely in terms of protective care into a period in which we recognize that it is very important for the older person to do as many things as he can for himself. It is what he does rather than what is done for him that preserves him. Hence, we encourage participation. In thinking of services for older people we think of temporary, part-time, and special services that will maintain participation and self-help as long as possible. In the modern design of institutions and homes for older persons and in the design of equipment, we return to a type of thinking that is common to much of our thinking about children.

With children we are interested in what the present can contribute to the future. We look to what the child will be doing three months, six months, a year hence. We expect him to find his way through the present to a solution and new skills in meeting similar problems in the future. While we as parents or teachers could do the job better, we let the child do it in order that he may learn. We believe that what the child does for himself is very important.

It seems to me that there is too much popular thinking about older people in terms that suggest that it does not matter what they do, they are going to die anyway, they have made their contribution to life, they are through. This is bad thinking about any living being. Life is a movement from the present into the future. Even though we are relatively inept and ineffective in the present, we become in a few months or a few years self-maintaining, independent, responsible individuals. I admit that this approach presents a real difficulty in the case of handicapped or overdependent persons. Our main difficulty is a limiting conception which interferes with thinking through the problem and seeing how to establish or re-establish the self-maintaining activities. It is perfectly proper for an older person to begin very complex activities and to start acquiring real skills instead of remaining passive and concerned with superficial activities at an entertainment level. Note, however, that I am not opposed to short-time entertainment and recreational activities. They have a real place in life, but they do not take the place of major and long-continued activities.

Conclusion

I have stressed as main points the need for continuing social relations and the contribution which the work pattern makes to them. We need to think of the human being in a context in which he is closely related to his fellow men. The second major point centered in the value of a work substitute or a major activity with which the older person can identify himself, which will have some kind of continuity and sufficient complexity to hold him over a period of time. I proposed that we examine our thinking about and our programs for older people in the light of this concept in order to see whether we really are giving older persons opportunities for self-realization. This ties in with the modern emphasis upon self-help in the design of housing, equipment, and services for older people.

Finally I mentioned the importance to society of developing ways to use the resources and capabilities of the older person. We are in a period of social transition when new roles and perhaps undesirable roles are thrust upon persons over sixty-five. How can we create the opportunities which will use their experience, skill, and wisdom and which will improve their personal adjustment while enabling them to contribute to the well-being of all?

ROLF B. MEYERSOHN
is research director at the Center for the Study of
Leisure at the University of Chicago. He was formerly at Columbia University in the Bureau of Applied Social Research and a teaching assistant in the
Department of Sociology.

Americans Off Duty

There exists a profound incompatibility between contemporary problems in leisure and in aging. Today's leisure patterns seem neither to influence nor to be
influenced by our older or oldest generation.

In the course of telling about America's prevailing
leisure patterns I shall try to indicate why this is so.

There is some question whether we can even use the
concept "leisure" to apply to the aged. Despite the many
confusions about the word, leisure is, in most of its usages,
set in opposition to work.

Definitions of Leisure

One use of the word leisure denotes time: time away
from work—evenings, week ends, vacations, holidays—
as well as time after work, or retirement.

According to this definition, there is more leisure than
ever. The working week, for example, has been reduced considerably in the past hundred years, and present talk about
the four-day week indicates that the decline is likely to con-

tinue. Our changing population distribution, the increase
in the population over sixty-five, has expanded the size of
our "leisure classes." In other words, as compared to the
past a smaller percentage of our male population is at work,
and they are working fewer hours. In this sense, then, there
is more leisure than ever before.

Leisure, however, calls for more than time alone. A
second definition distinguishes leisure from both work and
idleness on the basis of activities. We commonly assume
that only when a particular set of activities is pursued can
a person be considered "at leisure." These might include
sports, hobbies, games, recreation. Here, too, the statistics
show enormous increases; there is more participation in all
leisure activities than ever before.

But activities are not necessarily synonymous with
leisure. If I play golf and at the same time make a valuable
business contact, is this leisure or is it work? If I go out for
a business luncheon and spend the whole time talking about
my golf score, is that leisure or work? It is not easy to make
a distinction between the two on the basis of activities.

A third component must be considered, which might be
called a leisure attitude or state of mind. The concept leisure
is used largely as a negative one—off-duty time and nonwork
activities—but there is implied in it, vaguely perhaps, a body
of satisfactions and functions.

A current study of leisure, conducted under the auspices
of UNESCO, has labeled these attitudes and functions suc-
cinctly. They define leisure activities as: "Pursuits to which
each can devote himself according to his inclination; outside the demands of his work, his family, and his society;
for refreshment, diversion, or personal enrichment."

The release on this study goes on to explain that these

functions—refreshment, diversion, or personal enrichment—
"are effectively and often simultaneously fulfilled by leisure.
This list makes it possible to avoid certain pseudo-educational
prejudices which would tend to lead to a narrow control,
ignoring the real needs and aspirations of individuals and
groups . . . It also avoids prejudices of a 'commercial' type
which would tend to lower the leisure occupations of adults
to the crudest forms of enrichment."

I suppose refreshment and diversion have, to a large extent, come to mean amusement and escape, even though completely different meanings, such as contemplation, are equally
germane.

No matter how we define it, we think of leisure as opposed to work, and this is one reason why there is an incompatibility with problems of aging. Can we even entertain
the notion of leisure as a permanent state, as a full-time
affair? It is not easy. The purposes of leisure seem always to
have been linked to work, even though at different times
different cultures have had enormous range in their attitudes
toward the two.

For instance, and to simplify crudely, one might say
that in ancient Greece work was despised while the fullness
of leisure was considered the precondition for making life
worth while. In comparison, the medieval Church held that
work or labor was a penalty for the fall from grace; leisure
was approved only insofar as it could be clearly distinguished
from idleness.

Both these views are in contrast to the attitude that
is more directly in our own historical tradition, that of the
Protestant ethic, the view that in hard work lies the way to
salvation. In this tradition, leisure not spent in the glorifica-
tion of God is sinful.

In our own day it is probably impossible to make general remarks on the cultural setting for leisure; it is certainly meaningless to say that we worship leisure and abhor work or vice versa. Blurred as the distinction may be, however, we are certainly bound to some balance of our work and our leisure. For the productive individual it may be his work that sets the pace for his leisure. The routine of work is fixed, both in time and in activities, while his leisure is interstitial. It fills the gaps of time and preoccupation.

But what about the aged? For the retired, insofar as they are "people not at work" such a situation does not hold, and possibly the concept of leisure as we now understand it cannot be applied. In some ways it resembles the state of leisure among the unemployed, who may have all the time in the world but no real leisure. In the definition of leisure there is indeed a great confusion.

When we move from the definition of leisure to the question of how leisure behavior is determined, we also find that the role of the old is marginal. Leisure is an area in life striking in its lack of rules. Ideally, leisure is unobligated time which can be spent in any way one wishes. It is supposed to be refreshing, diverting, and enriching, and what set of activities provides for such qualities is to be a matter of personal taste.

Neither today nor at any time in the past, however, has leisure been quite as "free" as it is intended. For, as happens in all areas of life in which decisions are left to the individual, customs are built up, mores established, norms created. Values and behavior in leisure have been applauded and abused in a variety of ways in different cultures, but all have had some social norms connected with them.

Differences in Leisure

In our own past, leisure in terms of time, activities, and attitudes was very clearly differentiated for different groups. One could tell the rich from the poor, for example, by the amount of time available for leisure, by the kinds of activities pursued, and by the attitudes carried with them. The rich were known as the "leisure classes" and their activities reflected their wealth—they were entitled to pursue more private pleasures (many of which today form the basis of our mass media and public pleasures). Their attitudes could be distinguished according to the degree of enrichment as against escape which the forms and motives for leisure took.

Other lines could also be drawn very clearly: the leisure activities of women were considerably different from those of men; contrasts could be made between rural and urban leisure patterns; there were enormous regional differences, cultural differences, ethnic differences, educational differences.

Undoubtedly these differences were never completely rigid, but at least there was for all a set of clear-cut expectations. Some may have consisted of ordinary things, hardly to be called rituals, such as rural couples going square dancing on Saturday night, or men of the lower class meeting their drinking companions in local taverns every evening, or upper-class families exchanging lavish parties. Whatever the patterns, they were firmly set and the behavior of the members of different classes clearly established. As with all clearly established patterns, while they may now seem oppressive, they did provide everyone with the security of knowing what to expect.

In this process, the role of the old was to preserve existing patterns, to transmit them, to be the culture-bearers.
In a primitive society with its vast body of traditions, this
role may be most pronounced and the old most likely to be
revered. But even in our Western society as men grew old—
admittedly fewer did—they were more likely to become
patriarchs (and women, matriarchs). They reinforced the
customs and values of the society, the center from which
attitudes toward leisure and work proceeded.

For contemporary America no such center exists. Only
to a small extent do the traditional ways of acquiring behavior patterns still prevail—people do not do what their
parents did. Technological changes and social realignments
have been far too great to perpetuate such transmission.
Even our own parents did not necessarily have a rigid and
permanent pattern of leisure pursuits. The nineteenth-century Victorian pattern, the abstinent ideology, is now more
than one generation away, and a variety of social and political events has put it long out of mind.

Patterns of Leisure Activities

Some leisure activities are of course still characteristically upper class—fox hunting, for instance—or pool playing
at the other extreme. There are still regional differences and
ethnic differences; and the factor of education plays as great
a role as ever in the question of how people decide to spend
their leisure time. There are age differences; some activities
are popular among the young only—strenuous sports, for
instance—others only among older people. It is difficult to
find an example here, other than "playing with grandchildren." This difficulty points up a problem I shall come to

later, the fact that the current leisure is largely focused around younger people, leaving the old to their own—or no—devices.

Nevertheless, differences in class, region, size of city, and the like seem to be breaking down. Golf is no longer restricted to the rich, nor is tennis, and perhaps there will even be fox hunting on a mass basis one of these days.

Whatever the current patterns for leisure activities are, and the differences between groups in their pursuits of these activities, they are not so much determined any more by the presence or absence of facilities or money or education; instead, the major determinant seems to be interest or popularity.

There are indeed easily distinguishable patterns of leisure. For example, a study of a Midwestern community found very sharp distinctions between those teen-agers who go bowling and those who go roller-skating; almost none of the middle-class children went roller-skating, almost none of the working-class children went bowling—clearly not a division based on a lack of money or skill or access. It was strictly a social pattern, one that was determined by what might be called "peer-group norms" and that had nothing to do with any kind of long tradition that is embodied in the society and transmitted from generation to generation by its senior citizens.

Regardless of what leisure activities are pursued by whom, what is important is the change in the manner in which they are transmitted. Leisure has always been socially determined; but where, in the past, this determination was sustained by the older generation, and hence generational differences in leisure were relatively slight, today there are no comparisons any more of one generation with another.

Thus the older generation is isolated in the sense that it cannot help in the formation of new leisure patterns as they prevail in America today. The experience embodied in tradition and a long life no longer seems useful to the younger generation. While this is probably a perennial complaint of the old—and has existed throughout the history of man— it certainly appears to be truer than ever now. No matter what constant values may be found in leisure, they are not likely to compensate for the differences in the way our grandparents or parents spent their leisure when they were our age, or from the way we did when we were our children's age.

Changes in Leisure Patterns

The changes in leisure patterns have been of such a nature as to make the role of the older generation particularly sensitive and isolated. In our American society the differences between rich and poor, educated and uneducated, and rural and urban have not disappeared by any means. Nor are their leisure patterns identical. What has happened, though, is that the distinguishing features have been lost insofar as they were represented in differential leisure behavior. The cultural tradition in leisure pursuits has been replaced by short-lived and ever-changing customs, and these spread throughout our society. For the older generation this means that instead of relying on their experience and reserves of knowledge, they must struggle perhaps harder than any other group in order to keep up with the leisure of today, provided they care about being *au courant* about the leisure machinery as it is constantly retold by our Elvis Presleys and our other "heroes of consumption" (as Leo Lowenthal would call them).

These heroes of consumption are an important development in our society and have great bearing on leisure. They spring out of our mass media, whose growth has affected the traditional barriers in leisure. The mass media have provided for all a leisure activity which can be used for escape as well as enrichment, for gaining status as well as ignoring it, for obtaining help in one's vocation as well as one's avocation. They serve as a kind of blanket of leisure that has covered us all and has helped various groups—income groups, educational groups, age groups—to find out about one another. More importantly, however, they have provided a focus outside and external to any particular individual's age and class affiliation. In this sense they have provided a common denominator of leisure.

Common Denominators of Leisure

There are other such common denominators which, like the mass media, are not class bound, or bound by any of the other past distinctions. The automobile has permitted us all to travel along the same roads, to see the same sights, to experience the same kinds of sensations. Public parks and recreation facilities are unrestricted and owe their existence to the idea that the pursuit of leisure should be a universal right. The list could be extended; all of them have tended to reduce the differences in leisure patterns insofar as these differences were invidious.

While everyone shares in these common denominators, the old are not so much involved as are their children. Their enthusiasm for the mass media, for television, for instance, is no less than anyone else's, but they tend not to be the ones to determine what materials will make up the contents of the mass media. In the first place, program materials are determined by consumer strength, and as consumers the conjugal family unit is stronger than the retired. In a system of proportional representation of tastes, as the mass media are set up to be, any single group, such as the aged, do not have much of a voice. More than that, however, the mass media reflect America's dominant cultural values, and this country seems to be more concerned with youth than with age. The protagonists of most of our drama on and off the stage are youthful; problems of adolescent love and the conflicts of newlyweds—dating and mating—are considered far more interesting than most of the problems of the aged.

To some extent, then, the old are sharing in the common denominators of leisure more vicariously and perhaps more nostalgically than the rest of the population.

Other common facilities for leisure seem also to be geared more to the young than the old. The new "active leisure," as *Holiday* magazine calls it, is largely unintended for the old; the facilities of our national parks and perhaps even governmental allocation to recreational facilities are weighted in their consideration of youth.

Furthermore, most of these common leisure denominators are of recent origin. The older generation has no greater, and probably less, experience with them than their children and grandchildren do. They are not as "hep" in an age when our leisure seems to demand it. As culture carriers they have little to say when it comes to popular culture.

Constant Change in American Leisure

Perhaps the most striking aspect of American leisure is its constant change. Leisure activities move in cycles, in fadlike ways. Boating has swept the country, skin-diving

is suddenly popular, skiing has become a large winter business. These things get picked up at different rates by different groups in the population, and it may be true, as someone
has said, that by the time skin-diving equipment is sold in
mail-order catalogues, the people who bought it at Aber-
crombie and Fitch have long since stopped being interested
and are doing something else.

Such fluctuations of tastes in leisure pursuits can be
recorded for parlor games, sports, hobbies, and perhaps all
leisure activities. Shifts in Hooper ratings on television show,
as dramatically as any social chronicle, the irregular and
faddish nature of leisure interests. In some ways, the elements
comprising leisure tend to act much as radio and television
have acted in the past years. They have quickened the pace
of leisure fads. As the mass media have made and unmade
heroes overnight, largely because of their massiveness and
the speed of saturation, so leisure activities in general, simply
because they occupy a great deal of our time, develop into
short-lived fads. This is more than an analogy; as communication forms become more enveloping and immediate, very
few patterns of behavior, whether they be leisure activities
or anything else, remain private. Thus the mass media are
in part responsible for the quickening of the pace of fads
in leisure activities.

Such fads are likely to be of the sort that most older
people do not want to keep up with them even if they can.
Perhaps it is partly a myth, but it does seem that as one
gets older there is less interest in constant change and variety,
and greater desire for stability and regularity. Insofar as
leisure is currently characterized by change, it runs counter
to the predilection of older people. In this respect, too, they
seem isolated from the main stream of leisure trends.

Trends in Leisure

Of course trends in leisure do not consist exclusively of fads. Perhaps the most important phenomenon that is affecting leisure today is the migration to the suburbs; and this is hardly a fad. Here too the isolation of the old can be seen. Suburban living, while not a new thing, has tended less and less to provide a place for the older generation to exert its tastes and experience.

It is not because suburban leisure lacks patterns and even traditions. Some of them are, on the contrary, extremely rigid, but the kinds of traditions that exist are not embodied in the older generation. They are transmitted instead by the relatively young people who happen to have lived in a community longer than their neighbors. As William H. Whyte has pointed out in his studies of Park Forest, Illinois, and Levittown, Pennsylvania, the definitions of reality are man-made and made over in rapid succession by the new residents, who become veterans in the course of a few months or years.

What kinds of leisure patterns are they building and discarding? As a man makes more money and moves out of the city into the suburbs, what leisure habits does he drop and which ones does he take up? We can say right now that he is likely to garden, play golf, join a civic organization, become community-minded, school-minded, group-minded, and in many ways finds himself more rooted than he has ever been before. Social life in the suburbs does provide more visible links of identity that entail a completely different way of life. Everybody can see everybody else through the picture windows. Without delving into the whole question of suburban versus urban living—a topic which is not

at all irrelevant but simply one for which there is not time—
I want to mention certain shifts in leisure. These might be
called shifts of adaptation.

Adaptation to Community Norms

For men who do not have the background themselves
for easily transportable leisure activities, and must therefore
rely on larger facilities, the place of residence is particularly
crucial. More that that, however, the whole process of integration into the life of a community means adapting to
whatever prevailing leisure patterns are found. This does
not mean that private interests are no longer pursued but
that socially shared interests are added. It is not a simple
process of initiation by imitation, but one of slow adaptation
and adjustment to the norms of a community. If every neigh-
bor has an extensive garden, then the new inhabitant is likely
to take an interest in his. If all the wives on the block give
bridge parties, what brave woman will try play-reading?
Or vice versa. These things are not intended to sound me-
chanical; a number of things come into play because moving
to the suburbs implies by definition the acquisition of a
number of new goods and resources, including leisure machinery. All I am trying to say is that whatever is acquired
will be very much influenced by whatever has already been
acquired by other people in the community.

In such a process there seems to be little room for the
voice of parental—or grandparental—norms. Many of the
newer suburbs are communities in which everyone is, shock-
ingly, the same age.

Leisure activities also tend to be more homogeneous
in these communities and lack the diversity that a rich mix-

ture of age groups provides. Furthermore, the absence of older people means that there exists less opportunity for the present residents to prepare for their own future leisure by watching and sharing leisure with their elders. There is less room for what might be called anticipatory socialization to aging. For the aged this trend toward age homogeneous communities has perhaps led to the self-imposed isolation that some of our older people are taking on by moving to places like St. Petersburg, Florida. Perhaps this kind of solution provides for them an escape from the kinds of leisure shifts that have worked against their interests, but the loss to the rest of the society resulting from such segregation seems regrettable.

Conclusion

In conclusion let me review very briefly what I have said. I do not know much about aging and who is included in this category (though I suspect that the very labeling of the category for people who have many characteristics above and beyond the existential fact of age creates problems), but it appears that in a discussion of leisure this group is largely excluded. Leisure tends to be thought of in relationship to work, and for those who are no longer working, the complex equilibrium that exists in our society between work and leisure does not apply.

They are isolated also because of their alienation from the elements that seem to determine our leisure behavior; while in the past they comprised perhaps the single most important group for providing continuity in our social behavior, including leisure, changes in our society have led to the point where the past seems irrelevant. The area of leisure is particularly susceptible to the influences of social change. To some extent, leisure activities are picked up and dropped in fadlike fashion. For this reason too it seems that older people are isolated, because their interest in popular trends in leisure—many of which are applicable only to the hardy (like skin-diving, for instance)—is smaller than their devotion to more long-standing leisure activities. They do not often set the pace for leisure activities, and sometimes I suppose are not even invited to follow.

Perhaps the most serious isolation is occurring with the suburban immigration. Leisure patterns are created almost from scratch in new suburbs, and many are primarily designed for the conjugal family of procreation, as an anthropologist might call it, and few, if any, provisions are made for and by the older generation. In terms of one leisure ideal, namely the greatest possible diversity in leisure, such homogeneous communities seem particularly disturbing. Communities made up only of young suburbanites may be overly concerned with changing to the latest leisure fads; communities made up only of the retired may well atrophy from the absence of such a spirit. All in all age seems a poor way to stratify a society. While it is unlikely that the old will ever again have the same status as our major culture-bearers, it can be hoped that they will live in communities made up of all age groups and share equally in creating and enjoying our ever-growing abundance of leisure.

GEORGE H. SOULE

is a professor of economics at Bennington College in
Bennington, Vermont. For more than twenty years
he was editor of the *New Republic,* and prior to assuming his present position was a consultant and editor for the Twentieth Century Fund. He is the author
and co-author of many books, including *Prosperity
Decade, Economic Forces in American History,* and
Time for Living.

Free Time—Man's New Resource *

It seems advisable to approach the subject of
time as a resource from the point of view, not of the aged
or their special needs, but of reflections about changes in
our culture that concern all of us, of every age.

There is, too, a special reason why it seems inappropriate
to concentrate attention on the problems of aging before we
are in a position to judge to what extent these problems
originate from changes endogenous to human biology and
to what extent they arise from the social institutions and the
type of culture in which we live. Are we analyzing in the
right category the problems with which we are concerned?
Again and again, in the progress of human learning, it has
been discovered that scientists or philosophers have made
grievous errors or have run into insuperable barriers because
they began with faulty systems of classification, within which
they could not discover the truths most relevant to the puz-
zles on which their attention was focused.

I strongly suspect that many of the conditions which

gerontologists wish to improve arise, not simply because
a large section of the population has survived longer than
the rest, but because those who have done so are set apart
by a more or less meaningless label, referring to the number
of years they have lived. A basic difficulty, in other words,
lies not in age per se but in segregation of the aged both in
action and in thinking.

It has long been apparent to the judicious that racial
segregation rests not so much on meaningful differences between the individuals of one race and those of another as
on the fact that there is a crude and irrelevant classification
to which all such differences are usually attributed. Racial
segregation deprives its victims of equality in economic and
social opportunity because it substitutes a label for judgment of individual capacity and quality. Much the same
fate awaits those who, because of their chronological age,
begin to be classified, not on the basis of their personal qualities or abilities, but on the basis of what is expected of them
because the years they have lived have passed a certain
arbitrarily chosen number. A student of twenty who has a
bad memory is likely to rate a D in his course; but if a man
over sixty-five forgets something, he may be suspected of
senility.

So far as I have been able to discover, no expert in the
subject can put his finger on exactly what the essence of
aging is, either physiologically or psychologically. On one
point, however, nearly all are agreed—the differences among
those in any one age bracket are greater than those which
separate the younger from the older. If employers, for example, based their employment policy on this fact rather
than on chronological age classifications, it might lead them

to retire some workers at thirty and to retain others at one hundred.

The segregation of the aged is a large and many-sided subject, and it would be inappropriate to elaborate upon it before going on to my main theme. One further point, however, may be worth making. Segregation, which rests on a mistaken assignment of causes for difference through the use of a largely irrelevant system of classification, often tends to create in the segregated the very differences on which it rests. Even in his own mind the segregated person may come to regard himself as different because he himself tends to accept the common though fallacious basis of discrimination on which segregation rests. His experience in his social environment tends to reinforce this fatalism, which is itself a potent influence for deterioration. Often security may be gained only by surrender to the common judgment. On this account, we who are interested in gerontology ought, it seems to me, to be particularly careful not to reinforce the error either in our own thinking or through the very fact that our discussions imply a system of age classification. There is, to be sure, as much need for specialists in geriatrics as there is for pediatricians, child psychologists, and teachers and social workers who deal with the young; but, like the well-trained specialists in youth, they would be well advised never to abate their concern with the need to integrate their charges with the rest of the human race.

In a society like that of the United States, most people's lives have been centered about the production and consumption of goods and services. Mediating between production and consumption is a market, the operation of which is believed to allocate scarce resources in such a way as to provide satisfaction of consumers' wants, roughly in the order of their urgency. Resources thus allocated are customarily classified under one of three heads: first, land and its products; second, labor; and third, capital goods.

This account of our economic process is reasonably enlightening as long as the wants of a population are regarded solely as goods and services. We are paid for producing, and with the proceeds of our labor, we buy food, clothing, shelter, miscellaneous goods in almost endless variety, transportation, communication, education, and medical and hosts of other services. In an extremely poor society it may approximate the truth to say that needs for marketable goods and services are so urgent that all other wants are secondary. A starving or freezing man may scarcely satisfy or even feel any need except for food or warmth. But as availability of goods and services increases, it soon begins to appear that other wants are equally pressing. This ancient and trite observation needs no elaboration. Yet a commonplace often masks an unfamiliar truth. The wants or satisfactions other than those obtainable from goods and services indicate a demand for a scarce resource other than the trio—land, labor, and capital—which economists have recognized as necessary for production. This fourth resource is time.

Twenty-four hours a day are, by nature, the private property of each human being, even if he owns no land and no capital. In a free society he may—indeed, most of us must —sell some of these hours in order to buy the goods and services he most wants. For satisfactions other than those obtainable from goods and services produced for sale, however, he must keep some of his time off the market to use as he pleases.

Economists have agreed that wise allocation of scarce

resources is a major problem in their field of study. It has not been generally recognized that the allocation of time between paid work and direct uses by its owner is just as important as the allocation of natural resources, man-hours in industry, or capital. Furthermore, individuals have discovered again and again that allocation of time that they do not sell, their own time—"free time"—is an important problem not always solved with success. Scattered workers in the social sciences have in recent years discussed the importance of this problem, but they have not been able to devise a neat system of concepts by which to deal with it, like the market concept in economics, which is held to account for allocation through the interplay of supply and demand, costs and prices.

Leisure is not to be equated with idleness, especially not with the enforced idleness of one who is deprived of work which he would prefer to free time, either because he likes his job and the community of interests with which it provides him, or because he needs products and services which he cannot buy because his income without work is insufficient. Unemployment is not leisure. Neither is retirement leisure, insofar as it is not freely chosen by the retired. The concept of leisure implies the absence of compulsion to work arising from want of material goods and services. It implies free choice in the use of one's time whether for work or for play. A member of the traditional "leisure class" may indeed work hard at some self-chosen occupation. Many of the greatest intellectual and artistic achievements have been stimulated, not by commercial demand, but by the interest and dedication of men who could choose how to spend their lives because they did not have to make a living.

The relative abundance of material goods and needed

services determines, both for individuals and for societies, the amount of freedom that may be exercised in choosing how time shall be occupied. The striking increase in time off the job, achieved since the middle of the nineteenth century, has been paralleled by an equally striking increase in output of goods and services per head of the population. Without this gain in tangible income, the gain in free time would have been, if not impossible, at least unlikely.

The real net national product grew approximately thirteen times between the decade 1869–78 and the decade 1944–53. During these eighty years the population increased only three times. The real net national product per head of the population was enlarged, therefore, about fourfold, or at an average rate of about 1.9 per cent a year. In 1870 the standard work week was about seventy hours; in 1950 it was about forty hours. Working hours therefore were reduced about two-fifths whereas per capita income quadrupled.

If this same trend continues, material levels of living, on the average, may continue to rise while working hours decline. There is little if any reason to expect a diminution in the technical advance that has brought about the rising trend of output per man-hour. Indeed, the spread of what is now called automation seems likely to accelerate productivity.

One factor other than productivity, however, has contributed greatly to the gain in living levels and free time. This is the fact that the ratio of the total number of man-hours worked to the number of the population did not decrease over the long run—at least up to 1950—in spite of the drop in average working hours. While individuals worked a shorter time per year, the size of the labor force grew more rapidly than the population. In 1870 the labor force was about 33 per cent of the population; in 1950 it had become 42 per cent. Indeed, the gain in the numbers at work just about compensated for the decline in working hours. This left the population, on the average, able to increase its income of goods and services per head as rapidly as the output per man-hour grew.

The reasons for the growth in the labor force are found to a considerable extent in the age make-up of the population. A population with a large proportion of children under working age does not provide so large a reservoir of workers as one in which there is a greater fraction in the middle age brackets. In 1870 the birth rate was high, and the proportion of children in the population was large; but many of the children succumbed to diseases before attaining maturity. A fall in the birth rate, which continued steadily downward until World War II, combined with the conquest of many infectious diseases, resulted in a growing ratio of those between eighteen and sixty-five to those of other ages.

Two other influences tended to swell the labor force. Since 1900 especially, many women, formerly not earning pay, have taken jobs. And, from 1870 to 1914, millions of immigrants came to this country—a large proportion of them being men of working age, with few dependents of younger or older ages.

There is a limit somewhere to the growth of the labor force as a fraction of the population, and it is probable that that limit is now in sight, and perhaps has been passed. The birth rate rose dramatically immediately after World War II and has remained higher than since 1920. Immigration has virtually ceased. The fraction of women who take paid occupations may, it is true, continue to grow for a time. At the same time, the number in the age brackets above sixty-five is steadily swelling and may increase sharply if medical science should make as much headway in conquering so-called chronic or functional diseases as it has done in conquering infectious ailments. Meanwhile, more and more of those over sixty-five do not earn their living, partly because of the rapid increase of retirement, voluntary and involuntary. In 1890, 70 per cent of men sixty-five and older were in the labor force; in 1950, only 45 per cent.

Forecasts of future population are notoriously unreliable, but a few Census Bureau projections are striking. The number of women aged twenty to thirty-four, ages at which they are most likely to become mothers, has been high in the postwar decade, "is expected to rise moderately in the early 1960's, and sharply from 1967 to beyond 1975" in the words of the President's Council of Economic Advisers. In 1975 the number is expected to be 38 per cent larger than the high figure for 1950. By 1968 the number of children aged twelve will be roughly double that in the late 1940's. The college-age population—eighteen to twenty-four—reached a twenty-five-year low in 1955, but is expected to be 95 per cent larger in 1973—and undoubtedly more of them will go to college if facilities are provided. The number of people of sixty-five and over is expected to increase from 14.1 million in 1955 to 20.7 million in 1975. Their proportion in the total population is expected to rise from 8.5 per cent to 9 or 10 per cent. This forecast makes no allowance for possible changes in health conditions.

The upshot of these projected changes is that whereas in 1940 there were in the so-called working years (eighteen to sixty-four) about two people to every one under eighteen or sixty-five and over; by 1975 the ratio will be no greater than three to two—if we combine the highest projection of the "working ages" with the lowest projection of the "non-working ages." If these projections are not wide of the mark, a considerable part of any gain in output per man-hour will therefore be needed to support the increased number of dependents and must lessen gains either in material living levels or in free time to anyone else. Unless the demand for purchasable goods should cease to rise, or perhaps even fall, the outlook for further development of a leisure civilization might be retarded. To be sure, the gain in productivity by those with jobs might be so much greater than in the past that they could work shorter hours and still amply supply the wants of those regarded as too young or too old to work. Or the trends in population might be very different from those expected. In any case, however, it is about time to take a new look at the common assumption that paid work must cease at about the age of sixty-five.

These figures I have just cited indicate that retirement policies may be altered because a labor shortage will in the near future create needs for all of any age who are willing and able to work, excepting only those still at school. This is almost certain to be the case in education, as well as in other service and professional occupations. It is not likely that electronic devices can replace many teachers or medical workers, for example, without serious damage to the quality of the output—that is, educated and healthy persons.

It is well to remember that the rapid adoption of compulsory retirement, and the official encouragement of voluntary retirement occurred in the 1930's, when there was a surplus of labor. It was desired to take as many workers as possible out of the labor market and to find a way of providing an assured minimum of subsistence to those of the unemployed in the more advanced age brackets. The change

in the demand for labor which has since occurred has not
been registered in employment policies, and further pressure
from the labor market for appropriate changes, if it occurs,
may be fortunate.

Whether or not necessity forces the broadening of employment opportunity without regard to age, relaxation of
the age barrier is justified on broader grounds having to do
both with desegregation of the mature workers and with the
best allocation of our resources of time.

Whatever free time the economy permits is likely to be
put to better use if it is fairly shared among all workers or
potential workers, regardless of age, than if those under an
arbitrary age limit are compelled to spend longer hours at
the job than they would prefer in order to support in compulsory idleness those older persons who feel a need to spend
some of their time on the job, "earning a living." This is so
for at least two reasons.

First, it is in accord with liberal democratic traditions,
which assume that all have equal rights to life, liberty, and
the pursuit of happiness. Indeed, the Employment Act of
1946 places the federal government on record as bearing a
responsibility to seek such conditions that there shall be employment opportunity for all who are willing and able to
work. Both federal law and many state laws bar discrimination in employment because of race or religion. Why should
there be discrimination on the basis of age alone?

Second, the fruitful use of free time must be learned before middle life if those after middle life are to have a real
chance to spend their free time wisely. I need not describe
the calamity that awaits persons whose lives have been
bound up in jobs and who suddenly are cast adrift with few
interests and skills which seem to them—and often to others

as well—of the slightest importance. They have no leisure in the true sense if they have not freely chosen it, and any increase of their leisure would be unwise unless the free hours can have a value to them greater than that which these same hours would have had in the job.

Sooner or later, unless material resources give out or science and technology cease to advance, enough will be produced of marketable goods and services so that relative satiation of material wants for nearly everyone will be possible, at least in the United States. Already this is so with food, the market for which grows no faster than the population. It is beginning to be true with clothing. Housing is still short, but is more abundant than it used to be. The most rapidly growing industries, aside from those devoted to possible war, appear to be those that supply products usable only in free time, or those, like the food-processing industries, that save time and trouble for the housewife—and for the house-husband. By a process so slow as to be almost imperceptible, but nevertheless inevitable in the long run, a continual gain in capacity to produce consumers' goods per head leads toward a situation in which purchasers do not want to bother with more possessions of any one kind, but buy either for daily consumption or for replacement of existing articles, often by new and supposedly improved models. Even the markets for innovations have a way of becoming saturated from time to time. This is because a finite world does not offer space enough or, to any individual, time enough to care for and use more than a limited amount of goods and chattels. There are not likely to be more automobiles in use than there are roads enough and parking space enough to provide room for. In large metropolitan centers, the private motorcar is already going the way of the family horse—and megalopolis is almost here. There is not likely to be in any household more than one TV set per room, even if every member of the family wants to watch a different program at the same time. Even at much lower living levels than at present, workers have preferred more free time to a more rapid increase of material goods than they have received. This choice is likely to continue.

For the past century, working hours have been reduced by an average of three per decade and more rapidly than that since 1900. Even if the decline should become only 2.5 every ten years, the twenty-four-hour week would be here soon after the beginning of the twenty-first century. If the shortening of hours should proceed at the same rate as in the past forty years or so—four hours a decade—it would take not more than a hundred years to wipe out paid work altogether.

Naturally, this is not likely to occur. The tendency itself, however, implies broad changes in both economic arrangements and our culture, impossible to forecast in detail. What will happen will depend very largely on the choices people make, either as individuals or collectively, and also, of course, on the value judgments that determine these choices. It is already possible to discern a few areas of action in which such choices and values are likely to be decisive as to the nature and worth of our civilization.

The first is the choice concerning how the available paid work, and the income to be derived from it, are to be distributed. Shall we have in our highly efficient hive only a few specialized workers, a large number of drones who are supported from the common store, and as many queens as we think desirable maintained with scrupulous care only to perpetuate the species? Or shall the work, income, and leisure be as widely shared as possible, in the interest of a common satisfaction? At present there are tendencies in each of these directions, often in head-on collision.

We see the desirability of universal education and the need for extending it to more of the qualified at higher levels; this requires support of a large section of our population not yet prepared to earn their living and the subsidy of the educational services which they as individuals cannot buy. Yet we cannot seem to devise means of collecting from the active earners enough to pay the bill.

We know that many of the sick or feeble need support because they cannot work, yet our arrangements for collecting the necessary funds leave many of them in want. And, most fantastic of all, we deny the opportunity of earning to many competent persons whose only disqualification is their chronological age, while at the same time the savings, annuities, or pensions available for their use are, as a rule, not more than enough for basic necessities and often are less than that. In this case our own society at present seems incapable of choosing either the alternative of sharing paid work or of sharing the income to be derived from it.

The shift of emphasis from a market-centered economy to one in which free time is dominant must also be accompanied by a shift in values according to which time-use is judged and free time is allocated. The traditional attitude, inherited largely from the Puritan tradition, is that the real and serious business of life is work for monetary reward. The originators of this tradition regarded anything else as frivolous or indeed wicked. Little by little we have departed from that condemnation, as free time has increased. We still, however, often have a bad conscience about doing things for their own sakes rather than for economic sustenance or advancement, and tend to regard leisure as justifiable only for rest, recreation, or what are generally termed "hobbies." This word apparently is derived from the nursery hobbyhorse, which rocks back and forth but never gets anywhere and is a substitute for a real steed, which might be too vital for the rider to manage. If we throw off the Puritan tradition about paid work, it is often only to give it unconscious homage by resorting mainly to frivolous pursuits—or in some cases even those that are wicked—when we are not on the job.

We shall never be able to budget or spend free time with due regard to its scarcity value and with respect for human dignity unless we can develop much more fully and intelligently than is now usual a scale of values for time allocation independent of the market place. There are plenty of such values in our tradition. We can count numerous instances of great men whom we honor because they pursued significant activities which, regardless of whether there was market demand for them at the time, were immensely absorbing and valuable in themselves. There was no problem, for example, associated with retirement in the case of Benjamin Franklin, who gave up business in his forties—since he had enough to live on—and devoted his energies to scientific investigation and statecraft. Franklin certainly never undervalued the material things of life, nor did he undergo any sacrifice to pursue ends which seemed to him of greater interest than making money. I am not advocating the virtue of starving in a garret because there is no other way to paint pictures, write poetry, or compose music—though some will always be impelled to do that if it is necessary. What I am trying to say is that the richest civilization the world has ever known, and one that is growing richer daily, can afford to supply outside the market place both significant occupations and sufficient material means not merely to a few, but to many, if it will only take seriously the immense intellectual and aesthetic riches of its own tradition. It can build a culture worthy of respect if it will enable a large number of persons to be themselves in the best way they know, and to create in one sphere of activity or another, works that are self-justifying, and hence do not need the services of a Madison Avenue or an appeal to the lowest common denominators of corrupted self-interest.

If people are to have an opportunity to participate in rewarding living of this kind, it must be built into the civilization in which they have previously been conditioned. They cannot easily start all over again after a lifetime of activity spent largely in occupations which have seemed to them merely a grudging barter of time for goods that can offer them sustenance and perhaps status but little food for the growth of a complete and developed personality. A fumbling attempt of the superannuated to find something to do and something to live on in order to occupy time somehow until death claims them is in itself deadly.

It may be well to end with a few familiar but nonetheless true remarks on the role education must play if people are to be well equipped to live out full and long lives in a civilization in which free time seems destined to become more and more dominant. Obviously, though we may teach students how to follow what we flatteringly call a "vocation," education must give them much more meaningful opportunities than that. It must offer them access to the wealth of thinking and speculation, to the arts and sciences, that lie at the basis of the best in our culture. It must not be content to stuff them full of facts which they receive more or less docilely and retain only long enough to regurgitate in "objective tests," taken with grudging apprehension almost solely for the purpose of achieving the label of a degree.

The goal of education should be not so much to teach as to offer the opportunity to experience growth of the total personality, including, of course, exercise of the mind and the aesthetic skills. These are counsels of perfection, of course, but they ought not to be generalities meaningless in the daily routine and operation of our schools, as in many cases they are. If we can but produce a generation healthy and vigorous in both body and mind, capable of appreciating individual differences, and bent on seeking the best use of their limited time, when they are free of the job as well as when they are on it, we shall be practicing a preventive medicine which will make life much easier for the doctors, medical and social, who are concerned with problems of aging.

MAURICE E. LINDEN, M.D.
is the director of the Division of Mental Health, Department of Public Health, City of Philadelphia, and
the regional director of the Pennsylvania Common-
wealth Mental Health Center, Philadelphia region.
He was formerly the program director of the Gerontological Study Center at the Norristown Pennsylvania State Hospital.

Preparation for the Leisure
of Later Maturity

If the Aristotelian concept is correct that leisure is that which work has earned, then we must look upon
all leisure time as the reward of labor. Since we already
know that to many individuals enforced leisure is neither
sought after nor desired, we are confronted with the interesting philosophical paradox that the reward, leisure, is often
unrewarding. Undoubtedly this is owing to a variety of
sociological and individual psychological factors that seem
to be characteristic of our stepped-up and intensely busi-
nesslike American pattern of living. I am convinced that not
just the aging, but everyone in our society needs to learn
how to be leisurely. Not only because psychiatry is my spe-
cialty and interest but also because of the opportunity I
have to see the social casualties of our way of life do I conclude that the uses of leisure constitute a mental health
problem.

Since mental health can be measured only in terms of a

person's harmonious relationship with himself and with other people, it follows that an enriched sense of living, which is the outcome of appropriately utilized leisure, must be viewed in terms of social relationships. In this sense, however one fills his time may be regarded as an aspect of interpersonal relationship. Whether an individual is fishing from the bank of a brook in an effort to gain solitude and avoid contact with other people, whether he is touring the land to become acquainted with the customs and features of living of other people, whether he sits in isolated enterprise assembling his stamp collection secretly competing with other philatelists, or whether the individual is crocheting booties for an expected grandchild, in every instance either positively or negatively he is engaged in an interpersonal relationship.

I should like at this point to amend the title of my chapter to read, "The Preparation for the Use of Leisure Consists of the Development of Perfect Distance." Now let me explain this enigmatic title.

If I were asked what is the greatest single lesson in life that a child can be taught, my reply would be, "the lesson of the porcupine." A great philosopher has taught us that human social life is comparable to a group of porcupines sleeping on the ground on a wintry night. Should they roll together to gain warmth, they are apt to injure one another with their prickly spines. Should they then roll apart to avoid pain, their sacrifice of proximity renders them isolated and exposed to the chill night. We may conclude that porcupine comfort and contentment are to be found in their discovery of the perfect distance.

We may define perfect distance as a state of separation

that achieves warmth without intrusion and independence without isolation. Let us transpose this to human experience. We may conceive of a comfortable person as one who is warmly independent. When he comes near he neither nettles nor smothers. His love is without quills; his interest is without barbs; his self-sufficiency is compassionate and without estrangement.

In the public work of the Mental Health Division in Philadelphia, of which I am a part, we have attempted to determine what mental health is. It has been our studied conclusion that mental health is not only the relative absence of elements of personality that contribute to emotional, intellectual, or behavioral disorder, but that even more significantly mental health is the presence of those factors in human psychological make-up that provide for:

1. The capacity for selfless love of others.
2. The ability to initiate independent action.
3. The efficient discharge of effort.
4. The capacity for clear and concise thought.
5. A philosophy of group living.
6. A sense of purposefulness.
7. The enjoyment of the mere process of living.

Such elements are essential to good psychological health.

Now let us consider somewhat briefly in accordance with psychological concepts what the foregoing seven points mean in terms of mental health.

Selfless love is mature love. It means love of another individual for that person's sake. It means love with a minimum of personal gain in the process of loving. It is a state of giving and a state of shared experience. It implies making other individuals happy, being considerate, being interested, with a drive toward providing comfort and satisfaction. It is the highest, most civilized attitude to which the human soul can attain.

The ability to initiate independent action means untroubled belief in the social value of one's purposes. It implies the capacity for reflective judgment. It connotes a grasp of the requisites of an advancing civilization. It shows a knowledge of the qualities of living as well as the channels and avenues of worth-while social striving. It contains a comprehension of appropriateness of the products of experience and wisdom. It means an understanding of human limitations, one's own and those of others. It requires a disattachment from smothering external control and guidance coupled with a reliance upon one's own initiative and capacities. In the last analysis this is self-esteem without an admixture of deep internal feelings of inferiority or inadequacy.

Efficient discharge of effort implies complete psychological co-ordination or what we are wont in the humanities to call integration. It means that all parts of the human psychological and physical machinery are operating in unison. Freedom from suffocating inhibition and the ability to accept and correct one's own mistakes are integral elements in successful striving.

The ability to think clearly and concisely means that the mental apparatus, in its conscious day-to-day workings, is unhampered by insistent intrusions and interruptions from the deep-lying primitive and base instincts and drives. It implies a liberated mind capable of independent reasoning and perception. It means knowledge of the goals of thought and a logical process for arriving at such goals.

A philosophy of group living contains a socially appropriate understanding of moral and ethical judgments. It means understanding social laws and regulations not as arbitrary restrictions upon human behavior, but as an organized expression of considerateness for the feelings and needs of others. It means self-control and self-discipline. But even more importantly it means love of the race of man accompanied by a continuous sense of pleasure in being one of its representatives.

A *sense of purposefulness* contains two elements, a feeling of being loved, of belonging, and a set of goals in life in keeping with one's ability for achievement. It means the feeling of being a participant in a great creative scheme of realities. It means contentment with being a mere iota in an enormous mosaic pattern of human interaction and it means an acceptance of one's deficiencies, while such responsibilities are elected as are in harmony with one's actual personal resources as provided by nature. It implies a consistent faith in life as an indubitable reality containing a built-in aim of progressive change.

The enjoyment of the mere process of living is, of course, the sum total of all the psychological successes. This is tranquillity, a love of life unspoiled by inconsonance or doubt. The enjoyment of living without prolonged elation or depression is probably what we think of as happiness.

In our consideration of the main elements of mental health, we may find that we can fit them all into three psychological categories. One of the most important areas of the human mentality but the least accessible to direct observation is that vast psychological chamber that operates automatically and contains our forgotten memories. We usually speak of this as the *unconscious*. It is such nether regions of the human psychological apparatus from which energies of life spring and whence drives and instincts arise toward awareness. Most human motives start here and are colored by forgotten events from out of one's own historical past.

The second important mental province may be thought of as the area of self-awareness. In our professional lingo we call this the *ego*. It contains many levels of consciousness from immediate awareness all the way to the most dim and distant consciousness. We may simplify our consideration of the ego by regarding it as the mental apparatus that feels, remembers, thinks, associates one experience with another, develops intention and ambition, senses itself and the outside world, establishes purposes for action, initiates action, and evaluates itself through critical judgment.

The third important mental domain is that socially acquired psychological unit on which man seems to have a monopoly. This we call conscience, or in modern psychological terminology, *superego*. It represents the incorporation into the self of the images of people and personalities who have been important in an individual's life in the course of his development. This is the area of mind whence springs the realization of reward for good behavior and punishment for bad. This is the nature and demands of society internalized within the individual and personified in mental imagery. Such imagery consists of psychological representations of all of the people that the developing person holds dear and regards as his educators.

The manner in which the forementioned institutions of the mind develop is intimately dependent upon the kinds of human experiences the growing individual has and incorporates into his mental constitution. To the developing individual his parents, his teachers, his counselors, his playmates, his relatives, his peers and superiors, all of his social contacts and parentlike persons are virtually his educators. In a sense we are saying that man is a huge family and wherever the developing person goes he is in a home away from home, a school away from school. The great home, the world in which we live, is in fact the school of life. The purpose of the educational systems operating in the cosmic school of life is or should be:

1. To diminish the intensity of primitive energies in their primitive form.

2. To direct the mental energies that are freed in this process into the development of the co-ordinating unit of the human mind that we have referred to as the ego.

3. To provide the developing individual with the best possible authority and authority-like figures (parents) along whose patterns he may develop his own conscience and his ideals.

Recent social developments and experiences with our own problems lead us to the realization that the three most important psychological needs of developing people that are not yet being fully met with appropriate supplies are:

1. The need to reduce the tyranny of the profoundly located uncivilized and base strivings.

2. The need to develop ego structures capable of self-regulation and independent purpose.

3. The need to find authoritative figures in the environment that offer an ideal mixture of firmness, warmth, wisdom, stability, and understanding with whom the growing person can identify himself.

Errors are encountered in the process. The fortunate aspect of the train of living events is that so long as the person continues to be a developing unit he possesses the potential for internal psychological rearrangement. Errors can be corrected, provided that they are not perpetuated.

The most serious error in all of us, and perhaps the one that makes up the greatest problem with which we must all cope, is the human tendency to regard other individuals as extensions of ourselves. This means that the foibles, inconsistencies, and neurotic patterns which are our very nature are attributed to others. We may say that what we deny or overlook in our own psychological make-up we tend to punish in others. So often the growing person is rigidly disciplined and severely punished because we ascribe to him intentions, purposes, and ambitions which are in reality our own. The evil we see in others so often is our own projected evil. Another person becomes suspect because of our own bad conscience. Another individual is made to hew as a conformist to a line of training because of our own ambitions. The growing person's desire for independence is forcibly frustrated because of our own lack of independence as well as our envy of those who possess it. We think of the strivings of others as infantile because we have not grown up. We criticize or strive to frustrate others seeking after love and appropriate gratifications because we are unable to manage well our own identical impulses. We may be shocked at a person's aggressive and competitive drives because our own aggressive strivings are hamstrung and ineffectual.

It is readily seen that in a large number of instances we limit the growth of the maturing person not through social needs but because of our own personal unmet needs. This is what I mean when I speak of our tendency to consider others as an extension of ourselves. We have not achieved an ideal maturity so long as we have not effected a true psychological separation of ourselves from others. This realization contains an intriguing paradox. Excessive psychological closeness to other people renders us so intimate, so proximal, so near, that in fact we are unaware of the others. Thus, we see that excessive psychological closeness in which we identify too strongly with those whom we would seek to educate succeeds really in removing us to a great distance from them. When we misunderstand the needs and realities of other people we are remote. In such an instance we have in fact withdrawn ourselves into a state of isolation. The borders of definition thus become fuzzy between ourselves and others.

All that we have just mentioned much too briefly constitutes a human tendency that we may call defensiveness. When we are defensive we are too close or too far from other people. In this manner we demonstrate a cloying nearness or frigid remoteness. We have not achieved perfect distance.

In our society we seem to disregard our own logical conclusions that well-being is a relative state, and we treat well individuals with diffidence and dispassionate reserve. It is a pathetic commentary on the level of attainment of our civilization that we are able essentially to show a modicum of compassion mainly for the most helpless. In dealing with the so-called normal we place so high a value on individual striving and enterprise that we often tend to overlook and disregard our group obligations. Despite recent gains our social comprehension of public and preventive mental health is still primitive and undeveloped.

Some of our social leaders have recently pointed out that ours seems to be a sick society. It is an illness that produces a ferment and souring; perhaps we can call it dyspepsia of empathy, in which the milk of human kindness becomes congealed and inspissated long before it could give nourishment to the psychologically needy. While this applies to all age levels of people, the conclusion cannot be avoided that aging in our society is almost universally identified with emotional emaciation.

It is clear that we have an obligation to aid people in achieving what Dr. Bortz has referred to in some of his papers as a "maturing sense of living." The process of aging is normally accompanied by the progressive acquisition of special burdens upon the individual. Social aging to me means an increased sense of responsibility, a heightened appreciation of all forms of reality, a more pervasive feeling of sobriety, and a progressive obligation to make decisions. Certainly many people upon entering the mature years are excited by the new set of experiences and are stimulated by the challenge. Such people respond well to the calls of duty. Their personalities grow stronger as the potential of their real abilities and real talents begins to be reached. As such individuals go forward in life their enlarging egos increase the scope of their feelings and activities so that they are able to encompass many aspects of living in addition to the requirements of work alone.

Other individuals, however, when confronted with the great assortment of special obligations inherent in maturity, seem to lose courage early as their neurotic problems rise to prominence and hinder them from a realization of full attainment in the mature years. They surrender to unconscious pressures and become overwhelmed by anxiety-laden and conflicting feelings and impulses formerly held in a state of relative repression. For them responsibility may become confusion; reality may become a dream state; sobriety may be transformed into melancholy; and decision-making may become dependency.

Even for those who meet the challenge of maturity with strength and capability, aging presents special difficulties. There is ample reason to believe that leadership as a role in human society is based not only on the intrinsic worth of the person but also upon the special set of social circumstances he represents. We may say that leadership is institutionally based. It is not only what I am that may make me important but also who I am that may give me social status and prestige. When authority is institutionally centered, then removal of the individual from the institution with which he is identified constitutes a loss or diminution of the authoritative position. In this sense, then, any form of retirement, whether for a period of vacation or permanently after the attainment of a certain age, and whether it be from a business, industry, profession, social agency, or family structure, to many means loss, for a brief or great period, of an authoritative place in the social scheme of interpersonal relationships. Incidentally, this is a threat to more than the aging; it also constitutes a characterological deficit in younger people for whom the symbolic significance of the elder-authority becomes debased, impotent, and degraded.

As gerontologists we have a responsibility on a culture-wide basis to demonstrate that the concept of a maturing sense of living should apply to a philosophical value placed on social living itself. I believe that this value is being crowded out of the psychological atmosphere of our culture through the interposition of basically self-centered and materialistic motives. A youth-oriented society such as ours seems to have little regard for the set of values understood and appreciated by sagacious elders; and the elders' wisdom is for nought because it is either expressed in a vacuum or it falls on deaf ears. So long as the elderly are outnumbered, disregarded, and suppressed, their feeling for the depth of gratification that can be achieved in the enjoyment of the mere process of living must remain a minority viewpoint. Sociological studies suggest that the aging and the elderly are indeed a quasi-minority group. They are culturally excluded. Their suffering is all the greater, because their defeat may come at a time of greatest understanding.

Our efforts, therefore, have a twofold purpose: First, there is a need for effecting a progressive change in the cultural atmosphere that besets aging; second, we must prepare the developing person to develop in himself those strengths that will enable him to meet the exigencies, obstacles, and psychological emergencies of growing up.

If retirement from any other segment of living is to serve not as the withdrawal from all that has meaning but rather as the entrance upon the summit province of mature attainment and authority wherein self-esteem is conserved and mental health is preserved, then one of our goals consists of raising aging itself to the status of a desirable and prestige-laden institution. Aging must not be left to the mercy of the fluctuating tide of public generosity which floods and ebbs according to the gravity of social guilt and hysteria. It must be restored to succoring and invigorating channels within the main stream of living.

In the space that is left to us let us attempt to do the following things: Let us outline the various methods available to people to fill their leisure hours. Let us then relate such methods to mental constitution to demonstrate how the uses of leisure may build mental health. And then let us attempt to outline recommendations which, if followed, may enable people not only to prepare ahead for leisure-time activities, but also to make rewarding the reward of leisure.

I have studied many lists of leisure-time activities and have found that all of them may be classified into the following broad categories:

1. Some activities or services may consist of contributions to *social and cultural advancement.*

2. Many activities fall in the category of *creative expression.*

3. A vast variety of uses of leisure time consists of passive participation in what may be called *entertainment.*

4. The category of *recreation* is appropriate to the many forms of active and physical participation.

5. Much leisure-time activity eventuates in what may be isolated as a class having to do with *personal development* as, for example, reading and education.

6. Many leisure-time activities, such as working and playing with children and grandchildren, raising pets, and gardening may be thought of as a class of *fostering life.*

7. Energies are often directed into repair and renovation of a great variety of things and may be categorized in the class of *creative maintenance.*

8. A final category of human activities consists of *classification and ordering*—placing things in sequence or in pigeonholes.

Study of the foregoing groups of human avocations reveals that the following effects are achieved:

1. *Diversion.* The participation in a given activity in which an individual has a great deal of interest usually succeeds in taking his mind off himself. In the psychological sense diversion may be a counteractant against narcissism or self-centeredness.

2. *Expression.* Expression whether it be in the form of conversation, or as a productive yield in a creative sense

serves to counteract, nullify, and reverse feelings of frustration.

3. *Struggle for Survival.* Many leisure-time activities consist of intricate and complex interests that require the meeting of challenges and the overcoming of obstacles. Such activities serve to combat mental stagnation. Since it is known that there really is no such thing as mental stagnation and that a mind that does not go forward goes backward, the struggle-for-survival type of activity is a useful counteractant against regression.

4. *Creativeness.* The need to be creative is instinctual in man. Any activity that produces a creation is a desirable form of direct instinctual expression. Thus a creative use of leisure time is a method of liberating thwarted instincts.

5. *Membership.* Many activities are organized on a culture-wide basis. The participant who engages in this type of leisure-time occupation may well develop a sense of belonging to a group no matter how widely dispersed may be the members. The pursuit in such an instance brings the participants together in a psychological sense. Thus the feeling of belonging, even though the work is done in a setting of solitude, serves to combat feelings of isolation and lonesomeness.

6. *Participation.* Whereas membership may be defined as a sense of belonging, participation consists in playing an active role in organization. Such activity may provide that element of status and prestige that is sufficient to maintain a sense of self-esteem.

7. *Social Acceptableness.* While feelings of stagnation, idleness, and isolation may cause individuals to feel remote from the social group in which they want to feel they are members, hobby-crafts and other forms of leisurely diversion

are methods whereby the individual achieves a state of acceptableness. In this way feelings of being different are overcome and the individual may sustain the self-image of being "in the swim."

8. *Recognition.* The status and prestige that the products of leisure-time activity may achieve are direct antidotes to the toxin of cultural exclusion that embitters the lot of many aging people.

9. *Usefulness.* There is a tendency among people after their life's work is done, or if they think it is done, to consider themselves obsolescent, in the way, and useless. The development of a skill which provides a feeling of usefulness combats a sense of what I have been wont to call the "passé complex."

10. *Meaningfulness.* Many people in the earlier periods of life are so submerged in a workaday atmosphere of achieving economic security, that they fail to be aware of the world about them. Leisure often provides the opportunity for exploring nature. It is in such pursuits that the poetic and aesthetic values of life, life's meaningfulness, are experienced almost as a novel inspiration.

11. *Contemplation.* Leisure for individuals who desire to retain and foster the capacity for critical self-reflection affords an opportunity for self-analysis and self-understanding. This contributes importantly to the effectiveness of judgmental functioning, one of the real fortes of the older mind.

12. *Sharing.* Dividing one's bounty with another or others develops a feeling of mutuality and largesse which improves an individual's opinion of himself.

13. *Enjoyment of the Mere Process of Living.* When leisure time is filled with all of the elements enumerated be-

fore, it ceases to be just free time and becomes a way of life.

There are at least five recommendations that can be made to any individual to aid in his preparation for the employment of leisure.

1. Leisure should be set aside early in life and used as one is living. Through practice and application it can be integrated into one's own personal development and developed into a manner of living.

2. Individuals should be taught from their earliest days to develop some degree of routine without compulsion. When love is the reward for performance rather than the threat of punishment or retaliation, then the person in the course of living need not develop a compulsive drive, which is the defense against subtle guilt, hostility, and rebellion, but instead is freed to do things because he likes to do them and because he likes the people for whom he does them.

3. People should be encouraged not to be afraid to be silly or to make mistakes. As we know from experience with what is now called "brain-storming," many ingenious ideas have developed out of what appeared to be silly notions. Too many individuals possess a drive for perfection. Since perfection as a goal for human beings is impossible, people must be taught to reduce their expectations of themselves. This may enable people to be more flexible and to admit their errors. Every mistake admitted becomes the nucleus of a new ability.

4. It is desirable to impart the realization to people that they must be aware of their own limitations as well as the limitations of others. This also implies knowing one's strengths. Most important in this consideration is the realization of the extent to which an individual is his own authority.

This also implies an appreciation for the use of outside assistance and for what is beyond his own capacities.

5. People must be encouraged to alter progressively their culturally imposed attitude toward leisure, which is essentially one of guilt. Our compelling social need for income maintenance appears to have succeeded in making leisure both insignificant and wrong. There is good reason to believe that the cultural attitude here is in error.

In making social recommendations today it is found that decalogs enjoy widespread popularity. Let us add our decalog of recommendations to individuals preparing for the appropriate use of leisure in advanced maturity:

Continue to develop your resources. Popular dogma, which is incorrect to a considerable extent, maintains that the mental and emotional supplies of the human mind undergo a decline at or near the middle years. Recent studies strongly suggest that the reverse is more likely to be true. Psychologists have found that the human mind continues to develop its capacity for comprehending conceptual processes well into the seventh and eighth decades of life. The capacity for judgmental functioning and the integration of the human faculties that combine to create wisdom are still on the upgrade late in life. To be sure, certain physical and some emotional abilities, which were present in abundance early in life, tend to be on the downgrade in aging, but other qualities have not yet reached their highest developmental goal even in later maturity. In this respect you can think of the arrival at later maturity as the attainment of a broader outlook on life.

Increase your social effectiveness. One of the characteristics of growing older is the diminution that is experienced in the demands of the primitive instinctual drives upon mental attention. When such fundamental drives in life no longer mobilize human energy there is the potential for greater concentration and focusing of effort—a channeling of drives—with the end result of increased social effectiveness in almost every sphere of activity.

Enjoy your wisdom. One of the never-ending sources of deep satisfaction in the human mentality is the pleasure that is to be obtained from logical and reasonable behavior. The increase in sagacity and the values of the senior mind which are more in keeping with the realities of human life than at any other time in the life cycle can become the source of gratification formerly denied the youthful mind. In the young mind, the striving for self-satisfaction may blind it to the surrounding logic of nature.

Advance the tenets of human progress. There is evidence indicating that older people tend to become somewhat more conservative with advancing years. There is further evidence that suggests that this newly developed attitude in the older mind is of great value in conserving the indispensable ethical systems and mores that make civilization possible. Forward movement activated by men in the history of mankind has taken place largely through the cautious and understanding efforts of older sages. The development of the intellectual archives of our culture, the preservation of standards of behavior, and the thoughtful changes of social attitude that characterize social evolution have been conveyed from generation to generation by the parental figures. The desire for change and revolution in society is characteristic of the impulsive and tradition-destroying youthful mind which is often somewhat less capable of distinguishing desirable change from mere

change. The experience of the older mind, as a rule, gives it
an astute capacity to distinguish the good from the bad.

Externalize your interest. Researchers have pointed out
for many years that the young person, by virtue of the very
nature of his youth and the needs characteristic of the first
part of the human life cycle, develops an attitude of self-
centeredness and self-adulation. Such self-concern may so
occupy attention that the youthful mind is almost unaware
of occurrences about it. As the normal person grows older
he experiences a reduction in selfishness and develops an increasingly generous and altruistic philosophy which is considerate of the needs of other people. Such selflessness
removes the myopic prisms from the aging person's psychological vision and opens up whole new vistas of beauty
and natural grandeur which can be a revitalizing and refreshing experience in life.

Place your values in quality. The younger person has a
tendency, commensurate with his eager and aggressive nature, to place emphasis on quantitative productivity as a
be-all and end-all in human endeavor. The older mind values
the intrinsic quality of both things and people. Events and
objects which were formerly insignificant in life can become
a great new world for appreciation. In this sense hobbies
may become a rewarding avocation. The little things that
had formerly escaped attention become the artistry the emotional life holds dear.

Don't be a spendthrift of time. Time, the commodity
which youth wastes, misspends, and fails to appreciate, is
held precious in maturity. A well-spent hour can become an
eternity of pleasurable living.

Make your human relationships durable. It is well
known that the impetus of aggression and hostile drives

which tend to mar some of the enjoyments of life during the early years diminishes as one grows older. As an outcome, the feeling of love may become less tinged with emotional diversions. The love drives of the older personality, though less fiery to be sure than the passionate loves of youth, glow quietly and are capable of a greater degree of sincerity and genuineness. It is this quality of the mature person that gives him an unswerving devotion to people and to principles. If an older person permits himself to express this most desirable quality of the human psychological apparatus he has the capacity to achieve the friendships and more perfect love unions which have been his lifelong goals.

Don't capitalize on dependency. While the law makes it mandatory for offspring to accept the responsibility of the welfare of their parents, this should be regarded as an obligation only in times of need and not as a way of life. A poll taken among a large number of well-adjusted older people revealed that 90 per cent of them preferred to live independently of their children. They love their children, but they desire to be the masters of their own course through life and fate. Still, should tragedy overtake the older person he should not permit his pride and vanity to overrule his judgment and prevent him from accepting the support and strength that his environment makes available to him.

Exercise judicious independence. While the healthy mature mind has achieved the capacity for discrimination and reflection, such qualities can be utilized in assisting oncoming generations in becoming oriented to social requirements. There is an unfortunate tendency on the part of some older people to withdraw themselves from the currents of daily life, to hide behind a façade of resentment and remorse, and to thus succeed in denying younger people exposure to their wise deliberations. The older person should use his experience and accumulated knowledge aggressively, and thus assist oncoming family leaders in finding more direct paths through the vicissitudes of life.

The periods of maturity and later maturity possess the raw material out of which can be fashioned some of the most profound pleasures to which the human soul falls heir. Leisurely maturity can be an achievement.

One of our lessons in life is to be borrowed from children. Children do not play—they play at working. In their so-called play children solve problems, act out fantasies, develop aspirations, discover ethics, build relationships, and utilize all their resources. If adults were to make play out of their work, the transition from labor to leisure would be imperceptible. All living would be vital, relaxed, and socially oriented. The goal of personal well-being and perfect distance would be reached. If we develop and build upon the great number of resources with which we have been endowed by nature, we have the potential for an emotionally secure and gratifying future.

ROBERT J. BLAKELY

is vice-president of The Fund for Adult Education
in White Plains, New York. He was formerly on the
editorial staff of the *Des Moines Register* and *Trib-
une,* and was chief editorial writer for the *St. Louis
Star.*

The Way of Liberal Education

I am writing about growing old, of old peo-
ple—the old people we all are or will be, if we live long
enough. I am not writing of senior citizens or the golden age
or later maturity, or any of the other euphemisms with
which we Americans exercise our bent for verbal deodorants
to hide reality. We must look growing old straight in the face
and see it for what it is—a part of life—and accept it for what
it is, at the peril of not having lived.

I judge that most persons employed in the field of gerontology are in one or more areas of action or of research
pertaining to old people—not in education. My estimate is
that the present stage of action in this field is crisis, comparable to fighting a forest fire or combating a plague; and
the present stage of research is descriptive or operational
in the service of action dealing with crisis; and both are very
far indeed from the stage of affirmative concepts and activities, the equivalent to replanting in forestry or positive
health in medicine.

This is not surprising; indeed, it would be surprising if
it were otherwise. And yet there are dangers. A danger is

that this field of study and action will continue to be distracted by crisis; the "tidal wave" of students approaching higher education is as a comber compared to the rising spring tide of older people. The danger is that those who are in the field will become obsessed with the symptoms of empty later lives instead of dealing with the earlier causes of emptiness. The danger is that the field of concern will become set in the mold of therapy and social welfare, regarding being old as a necessary sickness, personal and social, instead of a part of a healthful life; regarding old age as a period of postdependency instead of the climax of independence. A danger is that we may become too successful in our palliation of the evils of the later years instead of making a radical—in the sense of "going to the roots"—examination of what is wrong with the values of our entire culture, including its education.

Most statements about liberal education are deductive from principles, not inductive from situations. That is, they reason, "Liberal education develops such and such qualities; these qualities are needed in all situations, and in this particular situation; therefore liberal education is relevant to this particular situation." They rarely reason thus: "In this situation such and such qualities are needed; liberal education develops these qualities; therefore, liberal education is relevant to this particular situation."

The deductive-from-principles argument for liberal education is not persuasive to most Americans. Why not? I suggest it is because in the United States we have not yet bridged the inherited chasm between liberal education and practical education. Liberal education is still identified with the aristocratic, with that which is not sympathetic to the everyday problems of everyday people; it is still deemed opposed to their interests—opposed or un-understanding; at any rate, it has not widely been translated as relevant to the concerns of most people. On the other hand, practical education is identified with that which is democratic; democracy is rebellious against that which went before, including previous educational philosophies; democracy is inclined to be uncritically optimistic, believing that forms and things and agencies are all that are needed; democracy is inclined to be undisciplined, believing that simply to want and to demand will bring the utopia.

I propose to make an inductive approach from the problem of old people in our culture. Let us be sure we recognize the crux of the problem. It is not old people and our aging population. It is that in our culture most of our old people lack the personal capacities to deal with old age; it is that our society does not have social functions for most old people. At root this is a problem brought about by changed circumstances to which we have not adjusted our education. Previously we had one kind of education for the few who governed and did not have to work for a living and another kind of education for the many who had to work for a living and did not govern. Now all of us share in governing; most of us have to work for a living part of our days for part of our lives but only part of our days and part of our lives. We have not yet learned what either liberal or practical education means in this changed situation.

In the United States we have educated and are educating quite well for working for a living, but we are betrayed by our inadequate education for the periods in which we do not work. Then we are like deep-sea divers brought suddenly to the surface. Let us realize how little of the time most of us work for a living. Multiply 365 days by twenty-four hours, getting the total hours in a year. Subtract 365 days times ten hours a day for sleeping, eating, and so on. This leaves us more than 5,000 hours. Multiply forty hours a week by forty-eight weeks, giving us the total working hours in a year. This gives us less than 2,000 hours. We are working less than two-fifths of our waking hours, and this fraction is constantly shrinking. This is for the working span of our lives. For most people after this span there is an increasing period of five, ten, twenty, even thirty years of no work.

In the United States we have not educated and are not educating well for the responsibilities of self-government in our private and public lives.

In our private lives we are getting an ever wider range of choice; for example, the choice of what to do with the time when we are not working. This is not free time unless we know how to use freedom. Leisure is not leisure unless we take command of it. If we cannot command it, others will command it for us.

In our public lives we are becoming ever closely inter-dependent with more and more people. The issues we face are multiplying and growing more complex. The magnitude of the stakes is growing greater. Yet most Americans pay little attention to public affairs.

How "practical" is an education which stresses preparation for work when we work less and less of our working span and live longer and longer after the span of work? How "practical" is an education which does not inspire and prepare most people to assume an actively responsible role in a society which has given the rights and responsibilities of self-government to all adults?

The consequences of this situation come to a head in

the empty later years—consequences in both personal tragedy and social danger: more and more old people living
longer and longer with no adequate personal philosophy, no
work roles, no social roles. Personal unhappiness can be en-
dured, but widespread social discontent is bound to be organized and exploited. This situation cannot be expected to
endure. We must remedy it—or face the consequences polit-
ically. We deny the franchise to young people because we
judge that they cannot perceive their interests. We may have
to consider taking the franchise away from old people because they come to perceive their interests too clearly and
too narrowly. This—or we must educate throughout life for
meaning and value throughout life, including old age.

Ortega has said that the greatest crisis of the twentieth
century is man's facing himself. I understand what this
means when I think of empty old people looking in the mir-
ror of social uselessness and seeing no faces or not liking the
faces they see.

The most impractical education is that which ignores,
slights, or takes for granted the meaning and values of life.
The most practical education is that which aids in the search,
clarification, and enhancement of meaning and value for
self and for society.

How did we get into such a predicament? Out of the
many forces impelling us I suggest four: the confusion between schooling and education, the idolatry of work, the influence of the culture that surrounds our schools, and the
cult of youth.

Thomas Jefferson was a democratic aristocrat. He was
of the aristocracy and believed in an aristocracy—not of
social class, family, or money, but a natural aristocracy of

"virtue and talent," whose members might be found anywhere in society. These, he thought, should receive a liberal
education for leadership. He assumed that the preparatory
liberal schooling would result in continuing liberal education
throughout life. His own education was lifelong. As he rode
his horse about the Atlantic seaboard, he would carry books
in his saddle pouches, tearing off and throwing away the
pages as he read. For the people not of the natural aristocracy he prescribed three or four years of rudimentary schooling—enough to enable them to conduct their private affairs
and to understand the issues as presented by the leaders, and
to choose among them.

The American people quite quickly rejected the idea of
any aristocracy, even a natural one of virtue and talent. They
added more and more years of basic schooling for all young
people—three and four; five and six; eight; we are now approaching twelve; soon it may be fourteen or sixteen. We
have assumed that schooling is education, or that schooling
by others in youth would result in education by itself in
adulthood. Schooling is not education. The end of schooling
does not mean the beginning of education for most Americans.

Why has not the "push" by schools started the "motors"
of most Americans so that they can "take off" on their own
education? I deny that it is because most are not capable of
self-education. They have different kinds of motors and different capacities. But all one needs to do is to study children
before school, noting their curiosity and their creativity, to
see that not only do we not do what we ought in most of our
schools: we actually seem to do something wrong—we dull
and deaden! Certainly we clutter up our curricula in a vain
attempt to teach during school everything the pupils will

need to know the rest of their lives—an effort futile in a dynamic world, a goal we would not set if we assumed the pupils had the rest of their lives in which to learn.

In our schooling and in most of our adult education we idolatrize work. I have already treated the arithmetic of this. Not only is this impractical; it also has two other evil consequences. First, by stressing specialization, it divides us and splits us up. Second, by stressing function, it makes us regard ourselves and others as performers of functions, not as persons. And we are empty persons and useless functions when our hours and years of work are over.

Our schooling of youth and education of adults labor under a heavy handicap in trying to educate liberally or to liberalize education—the handicap of the pervasive values of the surrounding culture. This culture values action above thought, the tangible over the intangible, things beyond people, and the immediate reward before the delayed reward.

And throughout is the cult of youth. As a people we glorify the decade between, say, sixteen and twenty-six years of age. Is it more sad to see children trying to look and act older than they are or to see grownups trying to look and act younger than they are? Our task is not just to restore old people to participation in our society. It is also the integration of the idea of growth, the essence of which is growing old, into our philosophy.

A corollary of trying to teach young people during the years of formal schooling all they will need to know the rest of their lives is to forget what the wise men of all times have known—that children and youths, however gifted or learned, cannot understand the most important things of life. This takes experience—not just raw experience, but experience refined and transmuted by reflection into understanding. I could start with several themes to illustrate what I mean. I will begin with a comprehension of the fact of death—not an intellectual concept but an emotional reality, not a sentimental but a visceral emotion, not death for something and someone else, but death for one's self and all temporal things. Most young people (some artistic persons are exceptions perhaps), though they "know" they are going to die, feel they are going to live forever or, at least, if they die, will do so at some time so astronomically distant that, like astronomical distances, it has no real meaning. At a certain time, which is different for different individuals (perhaps the late twenties or early thirties for most), an awareness of death comes over one like the shadow of a flying bird. Like the shadow of a bird, it passes. But it returns, and goes away, and returns. One must come to terms with this awareness— either deliberately burying it, in which case it poisons and festers; or deliberately accommodating one's self to the fact of mortality. I am not being morbid. I am being realistic. The accommodation is the recognition that life and death are inseparable; that life is finite; that life derives meaning from its finiteness; and that one must economize it, in the literal sense, by comparing values, choosing, and using well. There is room and to spare for religion and philosophy: questions of meaning and purpose, relationships and perspectives. Only in the light of these questions and the search for personal answers do other questions have meaning and are other answers possible—questions such as the relationship between the individual and society, truth, justice, freedom. Only in this context can a judge or parent be fair both to those he likes and those he dislikes. Only in this context

can a person understand himself and others. A middle-aged
parent with children can at the same time relive his own
childhood, comprehend his parents' lives a generation before,
and foresee his life in the lives of those who have gone ahead.
This leads me to the logarithms of life and learning.

You are all familiar with the logarithmic ruler—the ruler
that measures successive units, not by a fixed length, such
as the inch, but by a proportion: number one is twice two,
number two is twice three, and so on. Our lives are measured by a logarithmic ruler. Our years shorten as they extend.
Doctors speak of the "slowing down of the metabolic top."
All the vital processes of the body begin with incredible
speed at conception, like a top flung onto the floor, and slow
down throughout life until the top dies. By far the longest
unit of our lives is between conception and birth. The first
year is by far the longest year after birth. The second year
is by far the longest remaining year, and so on. As we live,
our years not only become fewer; they also become more
brief. Our sense of time is somehow related to the speed of
the metabolic top—related inversely. It is like a motion picture: taken fast, it plays back slow motion; taken slow it
plays fast. As children we can hardly remember one Christmas, one first flower, one first snowfall to another. As we
become older the yearly events crowd together. As older
people we exclaim, "Is it really June again?"

There can, however, be compensation. With systematic
learning, with the transmutation of experience into understanding, we can bring ever greater dimensions to the ab-
breviating years. We can live each year in greater height
and greater depth. We can—but only through self-education.

Our years become fewer and shorter whether we will it or not. They heighten and deepen only if we will and make it so.

What should be the subjects of liberal adult learning? The answer is simple—the major issues of human existence, such as life and death, space and time, the relationships between man and God, man and man, the individual and society, truth, justice, freedom, responsibility, war and peace. These and other such subjects need to be approached both directly in their own right for their relevance to living and indirectly from the problems of living. But to say that some mature persons are not concerned with such issues or that they cannot comprehend such "difficult" or "high-brow" matters is insulting, not compassionate. It is to deny their humanness. These subjects are too difficult and too highbrow for us all, but we must all grapple with them, in our own way and in our own strength, if we are to live as human beings.

The expressions of these subjects are the familiar categories of knowledge—literature, the arts, the sciences, both natural and human, et cetera. These are the themes of humans alive. Our audience waits. We must design methods and materials appropriate to adults and to the conditions and circumstances of particular adults. We must learn how to use and devise social situations in which adults can feel at home. We must learn how to use and appeal to strong motives—the springs that make people "tick."

Now I turn to motivations. I will designate four levels of concern. These are not "scientific." They overlap. The names are not the best, but they make my point.

1. The narrowly personal. Examples: family problems; money problems; status problems; work.

2. The broadly personal. Examples: the children's schools; affairs of business, labor unions, voluntary organizations; issues in the local community.

3. The concretely impersonal. Examples: issues of state, national, world affairs; inflation.

4. The abstractly impersonal. Examples: humanity; ideas in their own right, such as justice and freedom.

"Practical" education has stressed the narrowly personal primarily and the broadly personal secondarily. "Liberal education" has stressed the abstractly impersonal and the concretely impersonal.

We must come to recognize the impracticality of the narrowly practical. We must learn how to make clear the relevance of liberal education to the largely personal and to the concretely impersonal. The hope is that there will thereby be an illumination of the narrowly personal and an induction into concern for the abstractly impersonal.

Just as schooling is preparatory for education in maturity, education throughout maturity is preparatory for old age. It is too late to begin when a person is already old if his interests have withered and his capacities shrunk. He is then the helpless prey of the narrowly personal.

I will give illustrations of how appeals to motivations may be made to mature persons to engage in liberal education of themselves and others. The human relationships I will consider are: (1) parents and children; (2) husband and wife; (3) the individual and/or couple with the social values; and (4) the individual and/or the couple with the community.

1. In recent years the phrase "family-life education" has gained upon the older phrase, education for "child raising." The significance is the realization that more than the children have to be raised. The parents must grow also. They must understand not only their children, but also themselves, each other, and something about the world in which the family lives. Whatever other advantages they may give their children will not be complete if they do not give them examples of adults who are alive, curious, and responsible in affairs beyond the home and the job. Children must be helped to emancipate themselves from their parents; and parents must learn to emancipate themselves from their children. The failure to do the first is often the result of failure to do the second.

2. The wife and husband have individual problems of adjustment as they grow older that can be helped by education. One of the most bitter remarks I know is attributed to Mrs. Oliver Wendell Holmes, who commented, "Washington is full of great men—and the women they married when they were young." Wives need to be aware of the fact that oftentimes, because of the restrictions of their lives to the home and the stimulation of their husbands' work, there is a danger of a gap in their development—a gap the wife can bridge through education. Sometimes it is the husband who vegetates and the wife who advances. In any case, the husband needs to compensate with interests and interestingness for the loss of his hair and the softening of his muscles. Together husband and wife need to develop a world of concern and activity for the not-so-distant time when the children are gone.

3. Individually and together, man and woman must learn how to escape the great American "rat race" for more

and more things. With wants numberless and insatiable, with a great campaign by advertising to create and stimulate wants, we can escape from the maze only by setting bounds to our material wants. I remember the question asked by a steelworker during a conference in San Bernardino. "Once," he said, "I thought if I made $5,000 a year I would have all we wanted. I'm getting more than that now, but nothing has changed. The other day I got my wife a new refrigerator. She was pleased until her neighbor got a bigger refrigerator. Now she is more unhappy with the new one than she was with the old. Where will it all end?" The answer is, it will not end unless we make it end through placing our values elsewhere than in material things or the status they symbolize.

4. Disraeli once wrote a novel about the "two nations" —the rich and the poor. In America we are making headway in the production and distribution of wealth. But we are creating another far more dangerous set of two "nations" with regard to civic participation—the overworked and those who do little or nothing. In the United States much of our government is carried on through voluntary effort. This is not just an aid to self-government. It is self-government, and many of the resolutions to the dilemma between more centralized control and the neglect of problems lie in voluntary action. Of all the fields of endeavor in the American society, no other is so easy to enter or to advance in as the field of voluntary effort. All one needs is the desire and the ability— the desire, really, because there is place somewhere for every ability. Through voluntary activity the young person can gain recognition. Through voluntary activity man and woman can achieve self-expression and advance causes in which they believe. Through voluntary activity man and woman

can prepare to enter and then enter middle and late years with personal values and social usefulness. One of the most neglected and most important of voluntary activities is the promotion of continuing education for self and others. With old people crying for function—with every community and organization crying for volunteers to do things that need to be done—here we have two needs and two resources that can fit together like the clasping of right and left hands. But the meeting can be made only if before they are old, the old people have conserved and expanded their concerns and their skills. When this is done—and we all know old people who have done it and not-so-old people who are doing it— the two extremes in motivation I mentioned—the narrowly personal and the abstractly impersonal—meet like the two ends of a scroll: the old person answers his personal needs through an involvement in concerns of humanity, meaning, truth, beauty, peace. He is no longer narrow, and his needs are no longer impersonal or abstract.

Business, labor, agriculture, the professions, voluntary organizations and associations, the informal community, formal government from the locality to the nation, you and I and the entire society have a stake in the solution of the problem of empty, useless old people in America. The view I have taken and the approach through education, with appeals to strong motives from early adulthood to death— these suggest work and to spare for all these agencies and institutions—for you, for me, for all of us. Let us remind ourselves what we are doing, however. We are looking, not just at a problem, but also at human resources, not just at functions or lack of functions, but also at persons, not just at a job that needs to be done, but also at the fulfillment of personal and social life.

Let me make a special point about our universities. The modern American university is no longer a university, with, as the name implies, a oneness, a wholeness, and integration. It is not even a pluralism. It is an accidental congeries, a senseless agglutination. Some time ago I was given a Cook's tour of the University of California at Los Angeles. I understood better than ever before why the football team is so important. It is the only thing all the faculties and all the students have in common. When the modern American university finds its communality, its oneness, if it does, it will not be within itself. It will be within the individual student and out in the community, attending such pervasive problems as that of our aging population.

Schools and universities must help—indeed must take the lead. But the kind of education needed to give us meaningful personal and social lives from early maturity until the end calls for all of us in all of our many roles to pay attention to the educative implications and the educative possibilities of everything we do—for ourselves and for others. In short, the educative community.

When we educate—educate liberally—let us be aware of what we do. We release; we liberate; we emancipate personality. Let us not think that liberal education is a gimmick, a special kind of specialized education more effective for a particular purpose than a specialized education. The essence of liberal education is the evolution of larger loyalties and the dissolution of smaller restrictive loyalties; larger than businesses or unions or professions; larger than self or family; larger than nation or even humanity.

We should be prepared to hear and bear what happens, particularly if we have emancipated old people. Yeats somewhere says something like this: "A young person cannot be honest either with himself or with others, because he does not know himself. A middle-aged person can be honest with himself but not with others, because he has given too many hostages to fortune. Only an old person, in the shadow of the grave, can be honest both with himself and with others."

What are the prospects? Crisis. I remind you that the Chinese ideograph for crisis is a combination of the ideographs for "danger" and for "opportunity."

The danger is everywhere about us, of kinds and in scales not known before. The dangers not only include the possibilities of the willful destruction of the human race, but even its destruction "by inadvertence."

If man is not obliterated—and he is tough—this is only a mild solace. The next time man crawls out of the caves the road upward will be harder. Gone will be the coal, oil, iron, and copper easily accessible by means other than those available through advanced technology. And—if he does clamber up the cliffs—man will be facing the same problems we face today—with only the heritage of our bad example and with the debilitating argument of our failure, which the "realistic" and "practical" people of those far-off-future days will not hesitate to make.

Or, all that is past may be prologue: the lightning burning the tree, the wood fire kindled by stick and stick, coal, steam, oil, electricity, uranium, plutonium; the wheel, the lever, the internal combustion engine, the jet, the rocket; all this may be prologue to access to the inexhaustible energy of the sun and the inexhaustible materials of the sand and the sea; and knowledge of seer and scientist may be prologue to insights into how to release the inexhaustible creativity of human beings—all human beings—into a harmony of tensions calling upon all human history and all human cultures.

It may be that the human race will make the most drastic of all shifts in outlook, more radical by far than the shift from Ptolemy to Copernicus or from Newton to Einstein: a shift from an attitude of abundance toward human beings and of scarcity toward things, to an attitude of abundance toward things and of scarcity toward people, valuing human beings as our most precious resource, each and all human beings, and ourselves, as exhaustless possibilities to be explored from birth to death.

Even if the best happens, let us not expect relaxation. It is in the nature of life that an increased radius of knowledge lengthens the inner circumference of ignorance. The answering of a question of any importance raises other questions. The solution of a problem raises other problems or transforms the basic problem onto a higher level. Today, for example, man drives from city to city. A century ago the problem was man against nature. Now the problem is man getting along with man in cars of combined speeds of more than one hundred miles an hour, each driver depending on the other and on thousands of persons not present who made and repaired the cars, the roads, the signal lights, and the thousand and one other things that make up our pragmatic trustfulness in an age of philosophical distrust.

Danger or opportunity. Destruction or utopia. We should not underrate human stupidity or perversity. Nor should we underrate the irony of history. The future might be neither of these and yet both.

Medical science is working on the probability that the apparently ironclad limit on human life will be broken—that humans will normally live to the age of 125 or 150 years or longer. If this happens and we do not solve the problems of empty philosophies and social uselessness, it may be that the old saw will have to be modified to "the last hundred years are the hardest."

Remember the myth of Tithonus, sung by blind Homer in his "Hymn to Aphrodite"? Tithonus was the son of Lacedemon, King of Troy. He was husband of Eos, goddess of the Dawn. He was so beautiful she begged Zeus to let him live forever, but she forgot to ask for immortal youth. Zeus granted the request. Tithonus turned into a hideous old man, whom Eos had to shut in a chamber and, Homer says, "His voice flowed on incessantly."

For myself, the only thing worse than immortal life without immortal youth would be immortal life *with* immortal youth.

There is neither immortal life nor immortal youth for temporal creatures. Mortality is the price we pay for awareness. Awareness can be an agony as it is for empty old people in a society that has no place for them. Or it can be an acceptance of the necessity of mortality, a gratitude for life no matter how few or many the days and hours, a serenity after the battles of life and before the unknown.

If there is a temporal mortality, it is not literal. It is achieved, if achieved, through the transcendence of self, through the opening of one's concern to that and those beyond one's self, one's own, and one's time.

"He who loses his life shall save it." This is said in various ways by the high religions and philosophies. It is one of the insights of that which should be the harvest of living many years, summed up in that sibilant and resonant old word *wisdom*.

EUGENE A. FRIEDMANN, PH.D.
is an assistant professor of sociology in the Extension
Division of the University of Wisconsin. He is the
author of *The Meaning of Work and Retirement* with
Robert J. Havighurst and others.

THE GOOD USE OF LEISURE

The Work of Leisure

Work in leisure represents perhaps one of
the more curious and significant paradoxes of the middle of
the twentieth century. Man has the chance to retire, but he
seeks work. How did this come about? What is its significance? Is an age-old dream of mankind now on the threshold
of realization, with man unwilling to accept it?

Over 450 years ago Sir Thomas More in his *Utopia*
visualized the day when man would work a six-hour day and
a five-day week. Four hundred years later, in 1910, the
founder of U. S. Steel predicted that some steelworkers
would always work a twelve-hour day if steel were to be
produced. Today the average steelworker works an eight-
hour day and a five-day week. This is typical of the average
industrial work week and, moreover, today we hear talk of a
four-day week. Indeed, in some skilled crafts a thirty-six-
hour work week is already here. Within a lifetime we have
witnessed the growth of an economy and technology so
productive and so bountiful that the work week of man soon
promises to be half of what it was shortly before the turn of

the century. Indeed, the work week of man as foreseen in the *Utopia* of 450 years ago may now be at hand.

Equally as significant as the reduction of the work week has been the reduction of the work life and the consequent rise in the years of retirement. These are years in which man can live without the iron necessity of work. These are years of leisure.

The increase in number of years of retirement available to the working man has been dramatic. In 1900 the average number of years of retirement was less than three. In 1950 it had increased to six. In 1975 the average is expected to rise to nine years. And if retirement ages are lowered by this date a man retiring at sixty would look forward to spending an average of eighteen to twenty years, or nearly one-fourth of his life span, in retirement. Thus, the dream of yesterday has become the promise of today. Yet, oddly enough, we tend to regard yesterday's dream as a "problem" when it arises today.

If we examine the evidence of today's retirees, we find that only for a comparatively few has this promise been fulfilled. For some it has been an unmitigated catastrophe. And for a great many of those retiring it apparently has been something in between: a period in which they have enough money to get by on, but not enough to do what they really want to do; all the time they want, but not enough activity that seems to them to be purposeful; the general respect of their friends and community, but not the feeling that they belong or have a useful or vital part to play.

To understand their position one must consider:

1. The changing significance of retirement in the Western world

2. The rapidly changed and still changing position of the older worker in our society, and

3. A look beyond the immediate situation of the retired or the older person himself at the problems which our new-found leisure poses for all age groups in our society.

Do workers want to retire? Our evidence can be drawn from various studies conducted by the Social Security Administration, several university research groups, the Twentieth Century Fund, national opinion survey organizations, and a few industrial concerns who have surveyed their own employees on this question. The evidence to date is not conclusive and, in some cases, is conflicting; but a few rather tentative generalizations can be attempted:

1. Most of the studies have indicated that 50 per cent or more of the workers surveyed did not want to retire.

2. Insufficient income was the most frequently cited reason for not wanting to leave the job.

3. The majority of the workers, however, gave reasons in addition to income alone for wanting to remain; and about one-fourth indicated that they would want to remain even though they had sufficient income to retire on. These persons stressed the extra-economic significance of work in their lives. For them, in addition to a living, it was valued as a familiar routine, an association, a source of status and recognition, an opportunity for creative endeavor, and a purpose-giving activity.

4. Workers in the professions and the higher-skilled occupations stressed the extra-economic meanings of work more than did workers in the lower-skilled occupations.

5. Studies of attitudes toward retirement since 1950 have shown a consistently lower percentage of workers who

do not want to retire than studies made prior to 1950.

6. There is limited evidence to suggest that employees of companies with systematic programs of preretirement preparation conducted over a period of years have more favorable attitudes toward retirement than workers in companies without such programs.

It can be concluded, of course, that retirement represents a sharp break in the pattern of life organization for the individual and that separation from the job represents a major—and for some an insuperable—problem of adjustment. Indeed, some observers' comments on the earlier studies have implied that retirement is an unwanted blessing and that work, and not leisure, is the most desirable condition for man.

But before we accept this suggestion in full we want to examine further the evidence of change revealed in the historical sequence of these studies. We want to try to see if we can interpret the changing attitude toward retirement in terms of the more broadly changing economic and social position of the older worker, as well as in terms of the changing significance which the growth of leisure is having for adults of all ages in our society.

One of the hazards in discussing older persons is the tendency to lump them together as a single homogeneous group. Certainly we do not do this with middle-aged adults. We analyze their patterns of behavior and ways of life in terms of their income level, social class, occupation, nationality, religion, rural-urban residence, and other significant socio-economic variables. Yet the same highly differentiated and individualized middle-aged adult is too often simply classified as an older adult or as a retired worker once past the age of sixty-five. Our older-worker studies have been

deficient in this respect. Although some of them have tried
to interpret attitudes and adjustment problems in terms of
differences in income, occupation, and value definitions, we
do not yet have an adequate typology for the understanding
of the older worker.

Important to any typology would be a historical perspective that relates the meaning of retirement for the older
person to his rapidly changing position in our society. The
rate of this change is such that it would be almost futile to
plan for tomorrow's worker approaching retirement age on
the basis of our knowledge of yesterday's retiree. I would
like to discuss a preliminary and crude framework which
might help relate the manner in which the workers of yesterday, today, and tomorrow view or will view retirement and
leisure in terms of broader social and economic trends now
observable in our society.

The Worker Reaching Retirement Age before 1950

1. *Nature of the retirement process.* This is the man for
whom retirement represented a forced separation from the
job, either for the convenience of his employer—as in the
original disability retirement systems of the late nineteenth
and early twentieth centuries; or for the welfare of his society—as was characteristic of the spread of fixed age retirement practices during the thirties, which in part were intended to remove the older worker from the labor force to
make room for the younger man. Retirement often was a
catastrophe that befell a man against his wishes rather than
a period of leisure to be enjoyed after a lifetime of work.

2. *Economic position.* The retirees of this period are the
ones who have felt both the immediate and the delayed

effects of the Depression. Those who were eligible for Social Security received benefits averaging but $40 to $60 per month. Typically, they had no supplementary company pension or, at best, a small one, and their financial reserves had been depleted or even wiped out by the Depression. These are the people over sixty-five described in the 1950 census as having a median family income of $1,352. In this group 75 per cent of the individuals living alone had incomes of less than $1,000; and one-fourth were dependent upon Old Age Assistance.

3. *Attitude toward work and retirement.* It would follow then that work beyond the age of sixty-five was a matter of economic necessity, and retirement meant dependency and a marginal existence. It is little wonder that studies in the early 1940's showed that 85 per cent or more of this group regarded retirement as an unwanted situation which was being forced upon them.

4. *Social position.* These were the pensioners, the petitioners, persons cut off from the work structure of our society and frequently isolated from participation in family and community groups as well. These were once self-sustaining adults, reduced to a position of dependency, looking to social agencies to provide economic support, health care, and the opportunities for the simplest, most elementary forms of recreation and social participation. These were the persons for whom our golden-age clubs, day centers, housing projects, and care programs of various sorts were originally conceived.

The Worker Reaching Retirement Age during the Next Decade

1. *Nature of retirement.* This is the transitional man; the man who is aware of the problem of forced retirement

faced by his now-retired friends. But he is also the man who now has had some opportunity to prepare for retirement, to look ahead to it as a way of life which can be planned for.

2. *Economic position.* There are no reliable figures concerning the income of today's retiring worker. But we do know that almost all of these persons are now covered by Social Security and that a great many of them will probably be able to retire at or near the maximum rate. In addition, perhaps one-fourth of these workers are currently included under supplementary company pension plans. And they have now had a period of fifteen years or more of almost full employment, during which they have had a chance to acquire some financial reserve, whether in a form of a paid-off home, life insurance, government bonds, or other savings. Perhaps a not atypical representative of the industrial retiree of the next decade would be a General Electric employee retiring today who has had thirty years of service, whose wages have been around $4,200 in recent years, and who would then draw $246 a month in combined Social Security and company pension benefits. This is undoubtedly higher than the current average, but we can be sure that a sizable percentage of retirees in this period will have incomes of $2,000 or better a year. This level was recently described by a government study as representing a "moderate" standard of living for a retired couple. They can look forward then to a substantial measure of economic security, although they may still lack protection against financial emergencies such as costly medical bills. They will have sufficient income for the necessities of life in retirement but not much left over for travel and other activities to fill their leisure.

3. *Attitudes toward work and retirement.* There still will be some who regard employment past normal retirement age as necessary for basic economic subsistence. But

we will find an increasingly large group who would be interested in the labor market either because they wish to obtain supplementary income or because the extra-economic meanings of work have been so important to them that they would not want to leave the job regardless of their retirement income. For the group who wants to continue for supplementary income, probably a part-time job would fill their needs. For the group that continues because of the importance of work in their lives, the job they remain at must satisfy them in terms of its status, routine, or other values which they have stressed. Significantly, this group would also be transitional in their attitude toward retirement. It is now being presented to them as a reward rather than a penalty. The newness of this opportunity, however, is finding them unprepared and apprehensive as to its consequences. Perhaps this is what is indicated in the studies that show that employees of companies which have had preretirement programs of some duration accept retirement more readily than persons who have had no such preparation.

4. *Position in society.* This group is rapidly losing its stigma of dependency and will be looking toward society for participation as equals. Their need for supplementary income is not so great that they are willing to accept work of any kind or on any terms. Because of limited income they still must look to their communities to provide them with leisure-time activities, but even now are beginning to demand a greater voice in determining the type of programs offered and in governing the organizations designed for them.

The Worker Reaching Retirement Age after the Next Decade, 1967–77?

This is the man of the future, and the date of his arrival cannot be definitely predicted. Many of them are already with us, but the numbers and proportion will be rising steadily.

1. *Nature of retirement.* Retirement for this man will no longer come as a penalty for being old. Rather, it will represent for him an opportunity for the utilization of leisure. It will not have the newness and apprehension for him that it does for the worker today. He will have had the major part of his working life to prepare for it. And society should have crystallized its attitudes toward the retired man by this time and have defined responsible roles for him. The leisure of retirement and the status that will probably be associated with it by this time will have a strong positive attraction for him.

2. *Economic position.* Without trying to predict changes in Social Security and private pension benefits or the course of inflation, we can make a reasonable assumption that this man will probably have an income large enough to allow a fairly adequate standard of living. In addition, assuming that there is no major economic setback, he probably will have accumulated sufficient financial reserve to protect him against most emergencies and to allow him to travel and participate in a variety of activities to enrich his leisure.

3. *Attitudes toward work and retirement.* Since he will probably have a more adequate retirement income, he will, in all likelihood, be less apt to regard work past retirement age as an economic necessity. He will want to work only if

the job is required as a source of extra-economic satisfaction. He will have had, however, an increasing amount of leisure available to him throughout his work life and the opportunity to discover nonwork activities that offer the type of challenge and the sense of purpose which the man of today too often finds only in work.

4. *Position in society.* It is not unreasonable to expect that the status of the retired man in this period will be considerably higher than it is today. He will no longer depend upon his community for support or even recreation. He will have the financial resources to move to another community if his present one is not satisfactory. At the same time, as a consumer he will be sought by his community; and as a man who has had the opportunities of leisure throughout his work years, he may well have developed skills which his community will want to keep. He will be a free agent, sought after—rather than seeking—by his community, by industry, and by society.

We have viewed the nature of retirement and employment for the older worker as it has been changing in recent years and will continue to change for the next few decades. We described three historical categories of older workers— the man of yesterday, the man of today (the transitional man), and the man of tomorrow. We defined them in terms of:

1. Economic trends—in which work in the later years was first a matter of basic subsistence, then became a way of gaining supplementary income, and finally may lose its significance as a factor which impels men to work in the retirement years as retirement incomes become more adequate.

2. The changing nature of retirement—in which retire-

ment is shifting from a forcible job separation for which the worker was unprepared to a well-established and anticipated period of leisure at the end of the work life.

3. The changing position of the older worker in our society—in which the status of the older person is shifting from that of dependency to self-sufficiency.

4. The changing meanings of work—in which the extra-economic meanings of work become more significant as the skill and responsibility levels of jobs in our increasingly complex industrial system rises.

All three of our categories of workers are with us today. A moving perspective becomes imperative if today's plans are to serve tomorrow's needs. This emphasis of the character of tomorrow's retiree does not deny the economic necessity of work for the older person today or overlook the many difficulties he has in finding a place in the labor force. But our consideration might well focus on the much-neglected person in gerontological conferences—the retiree of tomorrow who is the middle-aged worker of today. He will be the one who will reap the benefits of the economic gains and the new leisure made possible by the unprecedented increase in productivity predicted for our economy—made possible by what is being termed the Second Industrial Revolution.

The following questions present themselves:

1. *Under what circumstances will he prefer employment to retirement?* We have already indicated that the extra-economic values of the job will be of greater significance to the average worker of tomorrow than of today and can act to bind him to it even though he may be able to afford retirement. But he also will have had the opportunities for increased leisure throughout a large portion of his work life

and may find leisure careers which would adequately replace the work career in retirement.

2. *Will the role of leisure in relation to work undergo a basic change?* Up to now our leisure as well as most other activities of our life has been work-oriented. Leisure is often thought of in terms of "recreation"—i.e., activities to be engaged in during nonwork hours which will refresh or "re-create" the individual so that he may be a more effective worker upon his return to his job. Otherwise it is regarded as idleness. With increasing leisure will new types of pursuits emerge—goal-directed, useful, long-term, satisfying in na-ture—around which man may also focus his energies and ambitions? Will work once again in human history become a means to other ends—as visualized in Thomas More's *Utopia*—rather than an end in itself. If so, what do we mean when we talk of "employment" in retirement? Are we re-ferring to activities engaged in solely for economic gain? Or can employment for the older person be long-term purposive pursuits seeking other goals?

3. *What will the consequences be for our industrial system if a large number of its most skilled workers are re-leased from the necessity of work?* This is a question quite different from the ones usually raised in discussions about the older worker. Will the time come when an industrial system requiring highly skilled workers of long experience and mature judgment is faced with the problem of losing some of its most valuable workers because they *prefer* to retire? How serious a loss would this be? What might in-dustry be doing now to prepare the worker for a satisfying role during the retirement years?

4. *How can we prepare the older worker for the new leisure of retirement?* How do we go about preparing the

man of today for satisfying leisure roles? Can we add "breadth to depth" as Professor John Anderson suggested? How do we go about adding competency in purposeful leisure pursuits of a man whose efforts have been devoted to learning one pursuit, the job, extremely well? How can we extend his area of competency? Can we turn his abilities to some further use to his community, his society, and himself when the economic need for work is no longer present?

LEROY WATERMAN, PH.D.

is professor emeritus of Semitics at the University of
Michigan. He is the author of books and articles on
the Bible and religions of the world. He is especially
well known for his interpretation of the Song of
Songs.

THE GOOD USE OF LEISURE

Religion and Religious Observance

The word retirement represents a life maneu-
ver that calls for considered preparation. Otherwise a sud-
den forced retirement, as on the battlefield, may easily become a rout, a debacle. Yet with due attention and foresight,
it can be a deciding asset to victorious living.

Retirement, to be accomplished most efficiently and enjoyably, may call for as much as ten years of planning. Such
estimate is suggested by the fact that preparation for many
professions requires that much time or more. And is not retirement one of the quite popular professions of our time? I
believe it may even be said that the profession at the moment
tends to be rather overcrowded in spots, due largely to mis-
calculations or to too much rigidity in timing.

It is well known in academic circles that certain university professors, who were retired several years ago, are
still teaching full time in other universities. This phenomenon
can be duplicated in numerous fields.

Among the many things that naturally enter into preparation for retirement, we are asked to ponder religion and religious observance. I consider the two as one item, since religion without observance is not religion but at most only a theory, and I am aware of no such thing as cold-storage religion.

In approaching this topic, I would like it to be understood that the subject is being discussed not as something that has been by-passed hitherto, and only now for the first time is to be seriously considered. That, as retirement approaches, might make it seem too much like getting ready for the Judgment. On the contrary I am thinking of it as one of those regularly functioning forces like finances, health, and housing. All of these and others like them, no matter how familiar and routine in character, take on fresh meaning and significance as the period of formal retirement approaches.

At this point, however, there arises a query. Is it true that religion is one of the regularly functioning forces like financing and housing, for example? The answer has to be "No" if labels are to be relied on. We know that a considerable number of persons not only on the other side of the Iron Curtain have repudiated the term religion as outgrown. We also know that there are many who flaunt the label, but who, by their conduct, make the term a byword. We know furthermore that there are so many brands of religion even under the name Christian, whose adherents are very willing to have no dealings with one another, that it is not immediately evident what the common denominator of this particular religion of ours really is.

In spite of these negative provisos and others that might readily come to mind, we are of the opinion that man is, nevertheless, incurably religious. This conviction does not spring from contemplation of the object of religion. This approach, alone, too readily tapers off either into theological complexities or into a degree of purposefulness on man's part revolving around a vacuum.

We find ourselves on much surer ground when we attempt to deal with the subject of religion, which is human personality. Personality like all other entities of which we are aware in this universe is something that is in rapid motion, which we are called upon to steer and to take the consequences, whether we do so or not. Not to make the attempt is not merely to face the hazard of drifting, but in the presence of a multitude of other personalities and forces all moving increasingly at high speeds in our time, the certainty of disastrous collision leaves no ground for life expectancy worth mentioning. The result is that if human life is to persist it has to be purposeful for survival, to say nothing of any hoped-for enrichment.

Wherein then does purposefulness in life find its most adequate room for maneuver? Only, I venture to say, in viewing life as a whole in relation to its total environment as conceived. Now this can be shown to be what religion in all its mutations and divergences, from its most primitive forms to its most enlightened expression, always aims to do, however far short any given example may fall of this goal. Furthermore, religion is the only life instrumentality that always makes this conscious attempt. This shows the soundness of the religious instinct and its vital, structural place in the human economy.

Nevertheless, a second query emerges at this very point. Granted that the above is true, what response will a legitimate and well-intentioned purposefulness on the part of man find in the total environment? Will it be favorable? Will it be neutral and indifferent, or will it be hostile and frustrating? As to the last, we may say quite confidently that if the universe were really against man, he would never have persisted so long nor progressed so far from what he once was.

There are those who believe and declare that the universe does not care, that it is entirely indifferent and neutral to all man's efforts either to hold what he has gained or to struggle upward. But if that be so, then it should give him no support to make that struggle and the moment he paused, he should sink back to the point where he started. This, however, is not what has happened. On the contrary, that total environment has tempted man to the unscaled heights. Instead of standing idly by and letting his struggle deplete what strength he had, it has made the struggle itself an excuse for increasing his existing strength. For every upward step made, it has brought into view fresh resources of power with which to climb farther.

If these things be true, then the universe is neither hostile to man nor indifferent, nor neutral to his strivings, but is found abetting and encouraging every weakest upward reach of man. And as surely as this is so, so surely not only will religion always persist, but the God idea as the highest concept of reality will never cease to be central to religion. This rests upon the fact that personality is the highest concept of reality that we know, and hence its presence as a dominant aspect of our total environment, which we call the universe, has its assured place.

But if God and the universe are for man's highest good, why has his progress been so slow and fluctuating? Why is evil allowed to destroy so much good that has been gained? That legitimate query overlooks the fact that personality cannot function without the quality of free will and choice, even when it involves a wrong choice, and all humanity, as man develops, becomes ever more and more an interacting whole that has to go up or down together. There is no part of it that can be preserved in isolation from all the rest, as long as that quality in man persists.

God's judgment in disapproval meanwhile must rest on every attempted advance that is wrongly conceived, no matter how devotedly and wholeheartedly it may be attempted. The early Israelites conceived that God was for them as a nation and against all others. Their utmost loyalty and devotion to this ideal could not have God's support and favor, but they had to face his disapproval and judgment, and it ended in frustration and disaster, because, as we are now able to see, it was conceived as too small, narrow, and distorted an ideal for God and the universe to approve or ultimately to tolerate.

In the later years, we are probably in the best position we can ever expect to be to view our lives as a whole in relation to our total environment. That is why religion is a particularly strategic asset at the approach of retirement. From such a vantage point we can see back farther with a calmness and a practiced judgment, which the stress and strain of earlier years did not and could not afford. From there too, we can also look forward and see more clearly than ever before in what direction the dominant trends of our lives are taking us and whether these appear to be valid or desirable.

What dominant form then will purposefulness in life take in this setting; and in what sense will it come under religion? As in all religions, the first thing religion will aim to do is to preserve the values of personality, for this is found to be what the history of all religions shows. This proves to be a constant, found in every religion of mankind. Indeed it is a kind of common denominator of all religions and it can be summed up in the single word "salvation," while the differences in religions can be summarized in the different forms under which salvation is conceived, plus the different means by which it is to be achieved.

In earlier times, the one thing deemed needful was that a powerful but changeable Deity should be appeased. Morality did not enter into the problem. We realize that this was and is not adequate. Not only could a changeable God change his mind and hence also his protective favor, but we also know that other persons can destroy many values that have already been gained. How then can the values of personality be preserved in our world?

Here we face the central problem of civilization itself and of man's continued existence as man, and never so manifestly so as in this particular day and age of our Lord. How can the gains man has made be preserved and assured, both as desirable ends in themselves and as the basis for further progress?

A given civilization has within it a certain measure of dynamic that aids in its perpetuation, but for the most part any civilization is mainly a containing vessel. Its permanence, its rise or decline depends fundamentally on the motivation of the personality units that compose it.

There is one universal test of any civilization. This is to be found in its degree of acceptance of the sacredness of human personality. This is a concept that goes back to the earliest stages of prehistoric man and actually marks man's separateness from the rest of the animal world. It is expressed in early man's reverence for the dead. Animals have no cemeteries, no mausoleums. Primitive man thus did nobly by the dead. Modern man has done much less well by the living.

The very phrase sacredness of personality, however, brings it under the aegis of religion. To conserve, to promote, and to extend it is man's most vital religious task for the future of mankind. There is no other agency in sight that can ever take it over, and religion has to go much farther with this task before humankind can be assured of an enduring future. The dread alternative that can come from a lack of this quality stands all too manifestly ready at hand.

Wherever color or caste or economics take precedence of personality as such, there a civilization is in jeopardy. How far religion needs to go in this matter can be seen from the fact that there are as yet no established civil rights that are universally accepted in this land of ours. There are no universally accepted human rights in our world, though steps are being taken in that direction.

If the sacredness of personality were universally accepted and practiced, there would be no race problem, there would be no problem of color. There would be no problem of totalitarianism in government or in economics. There could be no wars and there would be no crime.

Nearly 2,000 years ago, Jesus of Nazareth prepared the blueprint for such a humanity and the specifications for realizing it. Not too much attention has been given to it since.

But as for the observance of the above-mentioned aspect of religion, do I need to say more than that it means practicing it—and how? There are no special days or occasions for it, but every human relationship, every touch of one personality on another, anywhere, anytime, everywhere, at all times, is fraught with power to raise or lower the par value of the sacredness of human personality in our world. That is where this fateful problem for man's future is centered and where the victory has to be won or lost. It calls for no greater muscular strength and no prolonged physical endurance. In the later years, with more leisure, with more time for deliberate choice, this period may well be the most fruitful in our lives, in thus contributing to the total happiness and security of mankind. What greater reservoir of human happiness can anyone contemplate? Yet let it not be forgotten that dividends of whatever sort only accrue from investments, never from hoarding.

HAROLD H. ANDERSON

is a research professor of psychology at Michigan State University. His publications include articles and books on child and clinical psychology, personality, and cross-national research such as *Children in the Family*, *Studies of Teachers' Classroom Personalities*, and *Introduction to Projective Techniques*.

THE GOOD USE OF LEISURE

Self-Expression Through Creativity

The thought of creativity brings to mind in many persons the Mona Lisa by Leonardo da Vinci; the poems of Milton; the Thinker of Rodin; the lightning rod, bifocal lenses, and the Franklin stove of Benjamin Franklin; the telegraph of Morse; the telephone of Alexander Graham Bell; the electric light and phonograph of Edison. Creativity in these instances is associated with a painting, a sculpture, a sonnet, an invention, a product that can be seen, studied, enjoyed.

The product, however, took time to produce; it did not happen all at once. In the conception and the making of the product there may have been several attempts, stages, phases, transitions, failures, revisions. It is known that manuscripts have been revised; paintings have been painted over and rearranged. There are even unfinished symphonies. In this sense creativity must be thought of as a process; a process of planning, experiencing, acting by the person who is creating the product. Athena may have sprung full blown from the head of Zeus, but there are few concepts or traditions in history of instantaneous, complete, final creations of a product which ignore or deny the process.

It is probably true that creativity as product has been given greater attention or emphasis than creativity as process. The product is something tangible that can be seen or heard, and can be discussed. The process is often obscure, unknown, unperceived, unverbalized, even by the person himself, and therefore uncommunicated to others. In fact, neither history nor science has developed a method or means for recording or evaluating process, the struggle involved in learning, or in conceiving and producing an object of creativity. The product and the process are both important. Without the process there would not be the product. Without the product or evidence of achievement there might not be the motivation to sustain the process.

In most of the thinking about creativity, whether as process or product, there is an implicit value judgment. We all recognize the illustrations given above because in each case the product has been accepted; it has been found by the culture to be "good." There is a solid tradition behind the evaluation of the product; yet in neither art nor science do we find reliable criteria for this evaluation. The history of science reveals the scientist's blind spots in viewing and evaluating the "goodness" of the productions of his colleagues. The invalidity of contemporary judgments is found on the frontiers of all human disciplines. Fabulous sums are paid today for paintings by artists of an earlier day who died in poverty and scorn. Ghosts of persons burned at the stake by previous generations are sainted today with cold regard for the unfortunate individuals who are now being excommunicated. The cultural lag in evaluation of what is new and what is also good or acceptable is found as well among physicists, chemists, and psychologists. The big gap in dealing "objectively" with creativity is the lack of criteria for assessing the product of creativity.

The evaluation of the product has many other obscurities. We know little about the development of social acclaim. Presumably a painting by Gauguin had some meaning to Gauguin, some worth, some value, even when his colleagues were laughing at him and the market would not offer him a meal for his product. Artists, economists, philosophers, and psychologists cannot explain what happens in the transition from individual value by the artist himself (the satisfaction of self-expression) to a status of social recognition and approval. The evaluation by contemporaries has so often been reversed by a succeeding generation as to place upon contemporaries a great burden to justify any evaluation whatsoever.

Even if we could invent a correction for the time lag in our evaluation of the creativity of others the problem of evaluation would still be with us. There would be a kind of academic futility in discussing our subject, "Self-expression through Creativity in Aging Persons," if we had to confine ourselves to the Gauguins, to the Benjamin Franklins, and to Nobel Prize winners. Where is the cutting line for discriminating the top level of creativity from any other level of importance? Is it less creative at the age of two to make a mud pie than at the age of twenty to bake a cake? Is it possible that the process of creativity may be operating both at the age of two and at twenty? If we knew more about the process of creativity and if we could recognize it at two and at twenty, would the problem of criteria be simplified by identifying the process instead of trying to evaluate the product? To discuss creativity as process makes it possible for us to neglect for the moment the question of value and of social approval.

It is in biological creativity that we find creativity in everyone. In biology, creativity is a continuing process of emergence of originals. There are no two cells alike. There are no two persons alike. Each biological particle or combination of particles is unique. It has never existed before and will probably not be duplicated. Not only is each person different from all other persons but each is different today from what he was yesterday. Biologists speak of growth as having two essential aspects: differentiation and integration. This means that through differentiation the parts of the body become more and more unique in structure and function. Through integration they function in a progressing harmony or biological unity of purpose among the parts. As process, growth is an abandoning, a yielding, a giving up of an organism's momentary structure and function "as they are" for new structures and new functions that are in process of emerging. Biological growth is a continuing process of creativity. Creativity is thus universal. There is creativity in all forms of life. Growth is a spontaneous, noncoerced process. It can be only facilitated or retarded.

There is another kind of creativity which we may call psychological or social invention, whose product is not an object as such. This is creativity not with objects but with persons: creativity in human relations. Creativity in human relations requires intelligence, sharp perceptions, subtle sensitivities, respect for the individual person, and a personal boldness to explain one's point of view and to stand for one's convictions. Creativity in human relations requires individual integrity and an ability to work with others. Historical examples are found in social and political attempts to deal with differences. Magna Charta, the Bill of Rights, the Emancipation Proclamation, constitutions, bylaws and their amendments, codes of law, and city ordinances are examples of social invention. There are lesser examples of social creativity such as arranging car pools, keeping on good terms with one's neighbors, or helping them to discover something new.

In all recorded history man has struggled with two problems of psychological creativity. The first is how to be an individual; how to have ideas of one's own; how to learn from one's own perceptions; how to develop judgment based upon experience; how to think for one's self; how to be original, imaginative, creative, explorative, experimental, resourceful; how to be one's self; how to be spontaneous in behavior; how to have the freedom to act on one's own ideas, value systems, and preferences; how to grow and develop psychologically at one's optimum; and also, within this freedom, how to listen and how to learn from others. In attempting to be original and to achieve something new, it almost inevitably happens that a person's behavior conflicts with the needs and plans of others and with their values, biases, prejudices, misperceptions, expectations, and demands.

The second great problem that man has struggled with is the reconciliation of individual differences in desires, purposes, motives, goals, values, and actions. Individuals are different, but they must exercise these differences in such a way that there shall be the greatest harmony in the behavior of men. In order to maintain individual spontaneity one must give consideration to the spontaneities of others and strive to live in harmony.

Man's second problem, that of discovering, developing,

inventing, and achieving harmony in human behavior, is thus inseparably linked with the first. If man behaved in such a way that each individual could approximate his optimum of spontaneity and self-development, that, by definition, would achieve the greatest good for the greatest number. The greatest good for the greatest number implies the approach to some kind of optimum development, some maximum of individuality, for each member of the social group. Magna Charta, the Declaration of Independence, the Constitution of the United States are creative efforts of man to assure the maximum of spontaneity and of self-expression to each individual and at the same time to achieve a maximum of harmony in human relations.

Basically, creativity is developmental in nature. In order to understand creativity in aging persons we must understand creativity in the infant, the child, the youth, and the adult. We must know what the environment has done in the past to facilitate the development of individual creativity and what the environment has done to restrict it.

As in growth the two essentials of creativity are differentiation and integration, so in social creativity the two essential qualities are spontaneity and harmony. Spontaneity, we assume, is innate; it is a quality of protoplasm; it is of the very essence of life. Harmony must be learned.

The big question for creativity in aging persons is at what cost in spontaneity or self-expression have they learned to live harmoniously in their culture? Creativity through self-expression is another way of stating the first problem of mankind: how to be spontaneous, how to be one's self, how to have ideas of one's own. As civilization has developed it has been necessary to restrict the spontaneity of individual persons where such behavior might injure another. The Ten

Commandments, for example, are prohibitions. They represent environmental demands which require conformity. They are designed to secure respect for the spontaneity of others. In our culture, older persons have gone through a Victorian process which we have called child training or socialization of the child. Only a part of our cultural program of child training can be justified on the basis of achieving harmony in human relations. In addition to the Ten Commandments, aging persons of today found perhaps ten thousand additional environmental demands which became part of their socializing process. Many of these were prohibitions, restrictions, obstructions to the freedom, the spontaneity, the uniqueness, the individuality of the child. Most adults while growing up heard many kinds of "No! No!" "Don't!" "Stop!" "Shame!" combined with all kinds of threats of present and future punishment, loss of parental love, even loss of divine affection. The socializing process appears to have achieved more conformity than harmony, where conformity is defined as behavior low in spontaneity and harmony is defined as behavior high in spontaneity.

There is a universal spark in the learning behavior of infants and of preschool children. When they reach junior high school most children have lost the creative spark. Instead of leading lives of creative spontaneity they work as we have taught them, if they work at all, for gold stars and for other symbols of adult approval. In high school they dress alike, talk alike, behave alike, and, paradoxically, seek bizarre ways of preserving or rediscovering the waning flicker of uniqueness with which they were endowed at birth. As adults they will take jobs, try to amass fortunes, try to become successes but all according to accepted practices.

There are other things to consider in creativity as a developmental process. There are family, social class, regional and cultural differences in environmental tolerance of creativity at different age levels. There are also general cultural differences in environmental demands for conformity and environmental tolerances of creativity and self-expression. For the first ten to fifteen years in the life of the average adult, the culture tried to stamp out his originality, his uniqueness, his spontaneity, his creativity. Even so, in childhood and youthful years there was more freedom for him to be an individual than is permitted the adult. Social evaluation of the products of creative work is much more lenient and flexible for the child and the youth than for the adult. Among aging persons, a few will have managed to retain the creative spark of their preschool years, to look upon old problems with a new eye, to seek new experiences, to find satisfactions in small adventures into the unknown.

For the large majority of aging persons, creativity through self-expression will be difficult. In childhood and youth they not only had more acceptance but they received special training with relatively flexible standards in evaluating the quality of their production. As adults, most of them became conservative, afraid of making mistakes, afraid of new experiences, sensitive through buried and forgotten guilt feelings of their childhood blunders. In earning a living and rearing a family most adults have lost practice in being individually self-expressive. Few have had time to be explorative beyond the requirements of the job and the daily household duties. As retired and aging persons, large numbers will never again feel the glow of self-expression. Few of them will ever again achieve creativity by themselves.

Without some special encouragement and assistance most will not regain the spark of creativity.

We have emphasized the developmental process and have raised questions about both the potentialities and the opportunities for creativity at different age levels. When we examine programs of self-expression for aging persons which we regard as successful programs, we find both the goals of the programs and the attitudes of the personnel repeating the philosophy and the other qualities of the good nursery school. There is an encouragement of spontaneity, a variety of activities to appeal to any taste and to any level of school. There is a studied avoidance of environmental demands or of standards beyond those which are meaningful to the person himself. There is great regard for the process of self-expression and almost no evidence of traditional cultural evaluation. At the same time there is a high regard for the other members of the group and a respect for their individuality, too. If the same opportunities and the same values were offered the middle-aged, perhaps people would achieve the years of later maturity better prepared to experience the joys of creativity through self-expression.

ERNEST W. BURGESS

is emeritus professor of sociology and consultant at the Industrial Relations Center of the University of Chicago. His publications are numerous in the fields of the family, gerontology, and urban studies.

THE GOOD USE OF LEISURE

The Retired Person and Organizational Activities

Man has always been a social being. He alone of all the animals has fully developed communication. He grows physically, mentally, and socially from childhood onward in association with his fellows. In complete isolation he tends to lose his essentially human characteristics.

Among primitive peoples and throughout recorded history man has lived in social groups: the family, friendship associations, and the neighborhood. Any group of which he is a member tends to meet four of his basic human needs; namely: (1) a sense of belonging; (2) stimulating activities; (3) a schedule of events to look forward to; and (4) a medium of sociability.

Modern Man an Organizational Being

Man has always been a group being. But modern man is becoming more and more an organization man. This is the unseen but inevitable result of the shift from a rural to an urban civilization.

A century ago, before the industrial revolution began in the United States, a person might be characterized as a family man. The family dominated the economic and social life of people. The family was often a self-sustaining unit, producing much that it consumed. It was also a unit of production. The farm in the country and the shop in the town were economic units, with the husband and father as owner and manager and the wife and children as workers under his direction.

The small family was often an integral part of the extended family. The social life of married children and grandchildren revolved around the grandfather and the grandmother. This was the age of the pioneer spirit and of rugged individualism. The grandfather was revered and sometimes feared. He might rule like a tyrant or as a benevolent autocrat.

With the industrial revolution came the factory, the large city, and the development of large organizations, which tend to become ever larger units whether companies, labor unions, educational and recreational institutions, welfare agencies, or churches. People are no longer self-employed, they are employees. Men and women have to depend more and more on organizations and often on large organizations, to find work, to gain security, to play, and to worship. The family has contrasted in relative importance. Outside of an organization a person tends to be useless and impotent.

Retirement a Crisis of Aging

These economic and social changes have affected no age group so adversely as they have the aging. Retirement may be taken as embodying an experience that is disturbing to nearly all older men and more indirectly to many older women. Giving up employment, often under compulsion or by necessity, is a sharp break in an established routine and a blow to a respected and achieved status. Employment in such a work-oriented society as that of the United States is the center and focus of a man's existence. By contrast the home, husband, and children constitute the focal point of the life of most women. When children grow up and leave home the mother finds that she has been retired from a large segment of her existence.

The retirement of the husband from employment entails still other losses to him and to his wife. First of all there is a sharp reduction of about one-half in income, the average for all persons over sixty-five years. From one-third to one-fourth of the older people have incomes below the amount that in many states would enable them to establish eligibility for Old Age Assistance.

Second, the retired man loses his friends on the job with whom he may have been intimately associated for years. Often these represent his closest and sometimes almost his only friends. As the years pass his other friends are lost by death or by moving away, or he may lose friends by changing residence to another community. Often he finds it difficult if not impossible to make new friends.

Third, he frequently finds that his children who have left home have moved to other communities. Even those who remain have their own social life and little or no time for their parents. The aging father and mother may have to be content with occasional visits with their children and grandchildren and with joining them for Thanksgiving or Christmas dinners.

Fourth, studies show that older people when they retire

tend to drop out of organizations. Often resignation from an organization is an act of economy to save dues and other expenses involved. Sometimes the older persons begin to feel out of place or even rejected by members who are still working, especially by those who are younger. In lower-income groups membership for adults often is confined to church and to fraternal organizations.

The Place of Organizations in the Life of Retired Persons

A study of nearly 3,000 older persons showed the superior social adjustment of those who were active in organizations. For the great majority of older persons, the potential values of retirement living can only be achieved through participation in organizations.

This fact poses a challenge not only to aging persons but also to our educational, recreational, welfare, and religious organizations. They should seek to find ways in which they can attract and hold the participation of retired persons. So far only pilot efforts have been made. Research and experiments are necessary to find the pattern of efforts that will prove to be successful. For example, adult education is now confined almost entirely to younger and middle-aged adults. The needs of older people open up a new and fertile territory. So, too, does volunteer service by the aging in welfare, civic, and religious organizations.

Special Organizations for Retired Persons

Older persons should participate in organizations serving different ages, but, like all other age groups, most retired persons find satisfaction in belonging to groups made up of their peers. This fact is verified by the rapid growth in recent years of day centers, golden-age clubs, senior citizens' groups, and others by different names. Many of these have been established for older people under a variety of auspices. Others have been organized through the initiative of retired persons themselves.

No matter what the auspices, certain principles for the success of these organizations seem to be emerging. First, they must meet the needs and interests of older people. Second, they should generally provide a variety of activities to satisfy individual differences and aptitudes. Third, the older people should participate in planning the activities. Fourth, self-government that is real and not nominal will ensure greater participation and better morale. Fifth, professional help is valuable but it should be unobtrusive and surcharged with friendship. At present too few professional persons have had the training and experience to work successfully with older persons.

The Special Problem of the Lonely, the Shut-ins, and the Isolates

Three groups present a special problem to organizations. A considerable proportion of older people report themselves as lonely, especially the single and the widowed. Many of these are eager to join organized groups when the opportunity is given them. The shut-ins pose special problems that organizations need to diagnose, and each case should be considered the basis for determining the best plan of assistance. The isolates form the most difficult problem because of their unwillingness to associate with others. Each case needs careful study as a basis for experimental effort. Perhaps some skill, aptitude, or secret ambition can be discovered which can be utilized to develop association with the others.

The Advantages and Disadvantages of Organizations

So far the advantages of organizations have been stressed to aid older people to realize their potentials for retirement living. It must also, however, be recognized that organized groups may develop features that are unfavorable to human growth. They, perhaps by their very nature, often tend to become impersonal, rigid, bureaucratic, and authoritarian. When these characteristics are present they react unfavorably upon the personalities of their members. These unfortunate tendencies should be held in check. The ideal organization radiates informality, friendliness, and sociability. The key factor is generally the leader, whose personality, policies, and programs permeate the organization and determine its spirit and influence.

Conclusion

Organizations are necessary if older persons are to achieve the highest potentialities of retirement living. The groups may be small or large, but they enable older persons to find self-expression. Retirement is or should be the time in life when people have the freedom to find the fulfillment of deferred dreams or repressed ambitions or new objectives. It is only through and in organizations that most retired persons can attain these goals.

C. HARTLEY GRATTAN

has been a free-lance writer since 1925 and has contributed articles to numerous magazines and to the *Encyclopedia Americana*. He is the author of *Introducing Australia, Why We Fought, The Three James: A Family of Minds,* and *In Quest of Knowledge.*

THE GOOD USE OF LEISURE

Education for Understanding

Why should we argue for education in the regimen of the aging? Considering the laborious nature of the educational process—the fact that it is work of a difficult and trying kind—would it not be kinder, more obviously humanitarian, to suggest that the aging be allowed to coast into an intellectual quietism, to decline toward a vegetable existence? Perhaps it would, but the trouble is that we can never be sure that what seems kind is actually kind. Kindness is a highly ambiguous conception, especially if it is determined more by considerations of the heart than the head. The heart undisciplined by the head can lead us to a line of conduct that by a subtle transmogrification becomes a gross unkindness. Thus in this instance, our head tells us that it is only by keeping an aging person alert and alive to his potentialities and full of a desire to make use of those potentialities in a world prospectively rich in rewarding uses that we can promise him satisfaction. Common observation tells us—and some of this has now been recorded by students of aging—that the aging person who remains active gets the most satisfaction out of life. But as aging creeps up on an individual the relevant definition of activity changes. No longer does he feel like a strong man ready to run a race or play a fast game of tennis. His physical powers begin to wane. On the other hand, his mind continues to function at about as high a level of excellence as before and, indeed, with cultivation, some hitherto unexploited potentialities can be developed. From this it would seem to follow that it is to the utilization of the qualities of the mind of the aging person that his attention should be directed.

Moreover, as man ages, our assumption is that he is inclined to try to make sense of life in a new and fundamental way. The old imperatives, active for years, begin to weaken. His family has taken, or is rapidly taking, its final shape. The boys are launched on their careers; they are making their marriages and establishing their own households. The girls have pretty much decided whether they too will try careers or accept the ancient conclusion that, after all, the best career for a woman is marriage and a home. With these points settled, or on the way to settlement, and his own career approaching a climacteric, the compulsion of the values that have carried him so far in life begins to weaken. The tasks set for him by the values of our culture, and to which he has given joyful personal commitment, are nearing completion. The sense grows that a life has just about been lived and yet more years stretch before him. How can they best be employed?

When we offer the suggestion that education has a role at this stage of life we are not implying anything so limited as retraining or rehabilitation but rather are suggesting that this is the moment for the aging person to look around, as-

sess his personal potentialities, and try to define a set of
values relevant to the new situation. The program "Aging in
the Modern World" * is designed to suggest this necessity.
This is where education comes in, for in a large proportion
of cases—we are not suggesting that our prescription is universally valid—it will be discovered that the search for a
new life-orientation leads on ineluctably to the conclusion
that one needs to know more and to think more about life's
meaning and significance. Paul Tillich, the great theologian,
suggests that a state of valuelessness—technically, an-
hedonia, or "anxiety over the apparent meaninglessness of
existence"—is rife in modern society. Many people live by
the values imposed on them by society, not by personal
values, and when the social values lose their compulsive
character and the person is thrown back on himself, a crisis,
mild or acute, supervenes. We are talking here about such a
moment. A corrective of this condition, always supposing
that it does not take a pathological form better dealt with
by a psychiatrist, is education. For education as we are defining it is an invitation to take a close look at what the wise
men of the past and present have to say about the human
adventure and the role of the individual in it. We suggest
that at this time they take a look—or renew their looking—
at the distinguished statements of great philosophers, poets,
dramatists, fiction writers, and general writers; the expressive
creations of painters, sculptors, architects, and musicians,
ancient and modern; the characteristic presentations of contemporary anthropologists, sociologists, psychologists, economists, historians, or gerontologists; the objectives, methods,
and spirit of the physical scientists—all these can be made

* Clark Tibbitts and Wilma Donahue, Division of Gerontology,
University of Michigan, 1957.

accessible if they are properly presented. This is the road to wisdom.

It is one of the tragic features of our society that while we have been remarkably successful in prolonging life—we have invested a vast amount of capital in this effort—we have not been equally successful in building into our society reasons for appreciating the added years. This is in some part because we are adapted to a very great extent—by an orientation toward work—toward a career and its almost inevitable concomitant of making a home and raising a family. We have done a poor job of developing values for life-governance that are realizable best in the leisure time that is to an ever greater degree a by-product of our success at work, and which sometime in the sixties is now usually becoming total through retirement. What we are searching for is a way of using our leisure—specifically, in this particular discussion, the leisure that comes after our socially ratified life-tasks are completed—in a fashion that transcends mere diversion or fun and begins to be meaningful in its own terms and that in a way changes our evaluation of the meaning of work itself. I would be the last person to suggest that leisure should be devoted to work of a kind. I am not sufficiently a Puritan for that. Rather I am trying to say that a self-determined proportion of leisure devoted to meaningful thought about what life is all about and to the use of time for creative purposes that will give one a sense that life, even when not governed by the conventional work-values of our culture, is nevertheless satisfying and worth while. It is to make the later years of life more worth while that we suggest that attention be paid to education as an alternative to a mere vegetable existence or to the acquiring of a reputation for being a gay (but pathetically frenetic) old blade.

There is no fool like an old fool, you know. I am arguing against the development of a superabundance of old fools out of people who have the resources to be something different and better.

Underlying my remarks is the assumption that the life of the adult is marked by recognizable and definable stages. It is an odd fact that the psychologists are victims of fashion. For a long time they have devoted a great deal of attention to the study of childhood and adolescence. Lately they have been getting interested in old age. But there has not yet been a fashion of studying the stages of adulthood, least of all the life cycle of the normal adult. Some of you may recall the name of G. Stanley Hall. As a student at Clark College in the early twenties I used to see Dr. Hall on the campus; I attended the annual lectures he still gave to selected students, and I shook his hand on several occasions. Dr. Hall wrote a vast two-volumed study of adolescence, published in 1904, and a book entitled *Senescence, the Last Half of Life*, published in 1922. He also wrote a book called *Youth*, published in 1906, but he seems to have written little or nothing specifically about adulthood, that curious country bordered on one side by youth and the other by senescence. This just about typifies the state of psychology up to our time. Today the focus is slowly shifting. In the "Readings" for "Aging in the Modern World" you will find some excellent papers on what happens during the life cycle. In the volume entitled *Psychological Aspects of Aging*, edited by John E. Anderson (Washington, 1956), you will find a good deal of speculation about this matter and gain a sense of planning for the study of it in the immediate future.

But as things stand right now anything I can say about

the stages of adulthood is highly speculative. Nevertheless, I want to call your attention to two phases of the life cycle which seem to me, and a good many others, to have considerable significance for adult education. The first is not really our prime concern here. Sometime in the thirties, early or late, after training and education have been "completed" for the time being, the career started, the marriage made, the home established, and the family begun, men and women seem to reach a state which can reasonably be called normal adulthood. They have left adolescence far behind, they have passed through that hobbledehoy period ambiguously called "young adulthood" during which they are adventuring beyond adolescence but have not won full acceptance by adult society. It is at the moment that they are at last accepted as adults that we can regard them as likely candidates for liberal adult education or its resumption after the hiatus since college graduation. They now have some leisure, the hurly-burly of "getting established" is over, they are settling down for the "long haul" of adult life. At least it seems a long haul at its beginning, but actually it is but a period of twenty-five to thirty years, or about as long as it has taken them to reach its beginning. It is during this "long-haul" period that the heft of the task of career building is done and the family is raised. As it draws to its end, another definite phase of life draws to a close and a new phase begins. This new phase is that with which we have a particular concern, the phase called aging.

I do not guarantee the scientific accuracy of this sketch of the life cycle. In fact I have a strong feeling that it is too broad and rough to be truly accurate, but at least it is a better presentation of the matter than the bland assumption that life is all-of-a-piece between adolescence and final decay.

As we all know, psychology today is a house of many mansions and no well-known mansion in it is devoted to the psychology of the adult taken as a complete, or holistic, and normal human being. Yet in adult education, unless we are beset by the notion that we should take a therapeutic line as our primary task, we must go on the assumption that we are dealing with normal adults. My professor of education, G. H. Burnham, a man of Stanley Hall's generation, wrote a large book called *The Normal Mind* published in the nineteen-twenties. I still own my copy of it, for discussions of the normal mind are not yet too common, but characteristically it is largely concerned with the abnormal mind. We are victimized, in a way, by a preoccupation with abnormality to the point where we are rather at a loss to state even a private, rule-of-thumb definition of what we as individuals mean by a normal mind. A normal mind is a mind that is not obviously whacky.

Lately I had the good fortune to chance upon a really excellent book that falls logically into this place. I refer to *Becoming: Basic Considerations for a Psychology of Personality* by Gordon W. Allport (Yale University Press, 1955). I recommend it warmly to your attention. I am now reading another book, the argument of which complements Allport's line, with which I am much impressed, *Motivation and Personality* by Professor A. H. Maslow of Brandeis University (Harper & Brothers, 1954). Allport refers to Maslow and Maslow to Allport. It is along the lines on which Allport and Maslow are moving, I think, that a psychology of immense usefulness to adult educators will be developed.

Let me make, in succinct and schematic form, some of Allport's points and indicate where Maslow fits into the scheme:

a) Allport points out that American psychology is primarily in the tradition of John Locke, committed to the idea of the mind as originally a *tabula rasa* given its character by the impact of sensation and the crisscross of associations. He points out, however, there is another tradition, that of Baron von Leibnitz, which "maintains that the person is not a collection of acts, nor simply the locus of acts; the person is the source of acts." Allport's thinking is in the Leibnitzian tradition.

b) In the light of this, says Allport, "When we ask ourselves about our own course of growth such problems as the following come to mind: the nature of our inborn dispositions, the impress of our culture and environment, our emerging self-consciousness, our conscience, our gradually evolving style of expression, our experiences of choice and freedom, our handling of conflicts and anxieties, and finally the formation of our maturer values, interests, and aims." For a psychology of personality relatable to adult education these are the questions we want discussed.

c) We want to look at the evolution of personality in terms of "creative becoming" within a life style. ("A personal style is a way of achieving definiteness and effectiveness in our self-image and in our relationships with other people. It evolves gradually by our adopting a consistent line of procedure and sticking to it . . . Style is the stamp of individuality impressed upon our adaptive behavior.")

d) One measure of intellectual maturity, from this point of view, is "our capacity to feel less and less satisfied without answers to better and better problems." This means that within the life style and life cycle of the mature, normal individual there are moments when the problems of living challenge them strongly. We have defined such a moment, the moment when the sense of aging becomes fairly acute. This is a time when a search for maturer values than have hitherto ruled is decidedly in order.

e) All this is founded on the assumption that we are talking about a normal person. What marks a normal person? Well, roughly speaking, a normal person is one in whom growth needs clearly outweigh such basic needs as safety, belongingness, love, self-esteem. This is where Maslow comes in, for his chief interest is to investigate and define the type of person in whom growth needs predominate as, properly speaking, the mature, normal person.

f) Such a person will, it is obvious, respond well to the suggestion that any feeling of uneasiness about the predicament of aging can be exorcised by further growth, or a change in the pattern of one's answers. He is in no need of psychotherapy but rather is in need, if in need at all, of assistance in carrying through a reassessment of self and of "life" to bring into being a constellation of values in harmony with a new life status. On the principle that the more extensively a man is educated, the more he is aware of alternative courses in life, and of the values to be found in the alternatives, we found an argument for the renewal of attention to that education which places a heavy emphasis on value-evaluation and new and more relevant expressions of values. The values to which one gives allegiance, consciously or unconsciously, steer and select perceptions, judgments, and adjustments, Allport tells us. Therefore any mature acceptance of aging involves our values; and education which involves a critical assessment of values and alternative values fits like a hand in a glove.

For an understanding of what Allport and Maslow are really talking about I refer you to their books. Here I have but skimmed off certain ideas that seem logically related to our problem and have tried to make them intelligible without getting bogged down in a detailed exposition. I hope I have made clear their relevance to adult education at the time of life and of the kind we are discussing.

In addition to looking at the psychology of the individual we should view him sociologically. We should, that is, try to understand a matter which makes Americans exceedingly uncomfortable—his class position, not class in the crude Marxist sense, but in the light of the subtler variations played upon the concept by American sociologists. Until lately, to get any sense of what the American sociologists were talking about, it was necessary to read a long shelf of books and relate them one to another and to some standard of criticism as well as a person was able. Now, however, we have a very useful volume that does that for us: *The American Class Structure* by Joseph A. Kahl (Rinehart).

We can not enter here into the intricacies of the topic; we must be content with a few relevant remarks. In looking at an aging person with a view to getting an intelligent conception of what education can do for him, and of the education which will best serve him, we need to learn his occupation as an index to the social prestige he enjoys and as a useful key to the probable life style he has evolved or adopted. We also need to know something fairly precise about his education. As David Riesman has remarked in a quite different connection, "Education is the great correlate" in American life. When we have investigated our persons sociologically, even to the limited extent suggested here, we are in a much better position to define how adult education can best serve them. On the basis of education, occupation, personal prestige, and life style we can pretty well predict the relevance of the educational offerings available.

While education is to be prescribed for all persons becoming conscious that they are aging, it must also be taken into account that people function on a variety of levels. The problem of varying levels is a vexing one for adult educators. It raises its ugly head at every turn. Ordinarily, we plan and develop our programs without too much self-consciousness about levels, and let the programs find their own level. Usually, this means that we cater to the needs of the aspiring middle class. In the case of aging we know that people at all levels are aging and we really should try to satisfy all. The program "Aging in the Modern World" is an admirable example of a discussion program, but it will not satisfy the needs of all possible clients. The way is wide open for somebody to meet the needs of aging people at other levels. Who, for example, will develop a program for aging working-class people that is more than a how-to device offering ways and means of getting the most cash out of social security and pension schemes? Workers have minds too; they should not be steered to a vegetable existence; but who is going to take up the challenge and really do something constructive at this level about which, really, we know remarkably little. What does it mean, in terms useful to a person concerned with education for aging, that such a vast prestige-gulf exists between the middle class and the working class, a gulf founded in occupations and formal education, and certainly clearly expressed in the life style, and even reflected to some degree in the timing of the stages of the life cycle. I wish I knew.

Underlying all my remarks up to this point is the assumption, thus far unexamined, that the person beginning to age can still learn. Actually, I take this to be axiomatic and I assume that all adult educators take an identical view of the point, but some of those who join, or may think of joining, our programs may not be similarly convinced. It is amazing how persistent is the notion that there is deterioration of learning power as one grows older. The notion has high status in our psychological folklore. I need not do more than suggest that it is necessary to take steps to dissipate it, but I am going to share nevertheless with you some illuminating observations on "learning theory and classroom practice in adult education," made by J. W. Getzels of the University of Chicago in a lecture at the University College, Syracuse University. Dr. Getzels makes seven points, several of which are strikingly relevant to our discussion today. I use Dr. Getzels' formulations of the points, adding my own commentaries.

1. Learning depends on motivation. A prospective learner must have a disposition to learn and, if our earlier remarks are sound, he should be motivated by growth needs if he is to get the most out of the education we propose to lay before him.

2. Learning depends on capacity. You cannot make a silk purse out of a sow's ear, but you can make one out of silk. You must assess the capacities of your group members if you are going to achieve maximum learning for all hands.

3. Learning depends upon previous experience. "Insightful learning depends on cognitive reorganization rather than on the accretion of material by rote." Cognitive reorganization is quite a task at all ages, but as one gets older and the volume of accumulated experience mounts in quantity, the amount of cognitive reorganization that has to be managed naturally increases also. Experience may help or hinder learning. It is up to the leader to take advantage of the helpful factors and get over the hindering factors. Not all experience is luminous wisdom. Not all wisdom that is lacking in luminosity is readily or willingly discarded.

4. Learning depends upon perceiving relevant relationships. The idea is to get relevant units of experience and relevant units of new knowledge (that is, new experience) into satisfactory relationship, or in our case into a relationship that "solves" the problems posed by aging. Out of what he newly learns and knows he must construct a new synthesis or "whole," which will represent a constellation of values and ideas for action relevant to aging.

5. Learning depends on active search for meaning. This is often forgotten. Learning of a kind without much attention to meaning goes on all the time. But we must found our efforts on a search for meaning. Therefore we must allow

plenty of room for fumbling around in the search. The meanings the learner discovers in or through the programs we offer represents the net gain of the experience of participation.

6. Learning depends on evaluation of progress. This simply means that the clients should be posted about "how they are doing." This need not be done in report-card style of course, but neither should it be done so subtly as to escape notice.

7. Learning depends on satisfactory personal and social adjustment to the learning situation. You cannot expect a group of people who do not get along to learn much, or one that finds the chairs hard, the room dingy, and the leader a bore, to learn much either.

I have traversed these points in greater detail than they perhaps require because I find them strikingly relevant to the kind of learning required to extract maximum profit from the kind of education I am suggesting. I have suggested —I have, indeed, boldly advocated—that variety of education which is helpful in clarifying and deepening one's insight into the human predicament. Dr. Getzels' points relate directly to what must be done to ensure that a program designed for the purpose we have in mind has a reasonable prospect of success.

There but remains the chore of tying together the points I have successively discussed. I began by maintaining that a case for education for the aging person could be founded in the nature of the aging person, particularly his greater vigor of the mind than of the body. I suggested that within the life style of the individual, and his life cycle, there comes a moment of consciousness of aging at which a re-examination and redefinition of values seems called for. I showed an enthusiasm for the speculations of psychologists like Allport and Maslow about the whole person and particularly the normal person seeking expression of growth needs. I suggested that certain sociological criteria should be applied to the persons one proposes to expose to education, the better to differentiate both them and the education offered. And I examined certain points about learning which, in most instances, are pretty obviously related to the educational results desired.

Index

GROWING OLD

An Arno Press Collection

Birren, James E., et al., editors. **Human Aging.** 1963

Birren, James E., editor. **Relations of Development and Aging.** 1964

Breckinridge, Elizabeth L. **Effective Use of Older Workers.** 1953

Brennan, Michael J., Philip Taft, and Mark Schupack. **The Economics of Age.** 1967

Cabot, Natalie H. **You Can't Count On Dying.** 1961

Clark, F. Le Gros. **Growing Old in a Mechanized World.** 1960

Clark, Margaret and Barbara G. Anderson. **Culture and Aging.** 1967

Crook, G[uy] H[amilton] and Martin Heinstein. **The Older Worker in Industry.** 1958

Derber, Milton, editor. **Aged and Society.** 1950

Donahue, Wilma, et al., editors. **Free Time.** 1958

Donahue, Wilma and Clark Tibbitts, editors. **New Frontiers of Aging.** 1957

Havighurst, Robert J. and Ruth Albrecht. **Older People.** 1953

International Association of Gerontology. **Old Age in the Modern World.** 1955

Kaplan, Oscar J., editor. **Mental Disorders in Later Life.** 1956

Kutner, Bernard, et al. **Five Hundred Over Sixty.** 1956

Lowenthal, Marjorie F. **Lives in Distress.** 1964

Munnichs, J.M.A. **Old Age and Finitude.** 1966

Nassau, Mabel L. **Old Age Poverty in Greenwich Village.** 1915

National Association of Social Workers. **Social Group Work with Older People.** 1963

Neugarten, Bernice L., et al. **Personality in Middle and Late Life.** 1964

Orton, Job. **Discourses to the Aged.** 1801

Pinner, Frank A., Paul Jacobs, and Philip Selznick. **Old Age and Political Behavior.** 1959

Reichard, Suzanne, Florine Livson and Paul G. Peterson. **Aging and Personality**. 1962

Rowntree, B. Seebohm. **Old People**. 1947

Rubinow, I[saac] M[ax]., editor. **Care of the Aged**. 1931

Shanas, Ethel. **The Health of Older People**. 1962

Shanas, Ethel, et al. **Old People in Three Industrial Societies**. 1968

Sheldon, J[oseph] H. **The Social Medicine of Old Age**. 1948

Shock, N[athan] W., editor. **Perspectives in Experimental Gerontology**. 1966

Tibbitts, Clark, editor. **Social Contribution by the Aging**. 1952

Tibbitts, Clark and Wilma Donahue, editors. **Social and Psychological Aspects of Aging**. 1962

U.S. Dept. of Health, Education, and Welfare. **Working With Older People**. 1970

Vischer, A[dolf] L[ucas]. **Old Age**. 1947

Welford, A[lan] T[raviss], and James E. Birren, editors. **Decision Making and Age**. 1969

Williams, Richard H., Clark Tibbitts, and Wilma Donahue, editors. **Processes of Aging**. 1963